Forbidden Fruit
an LGBT
18+ zine

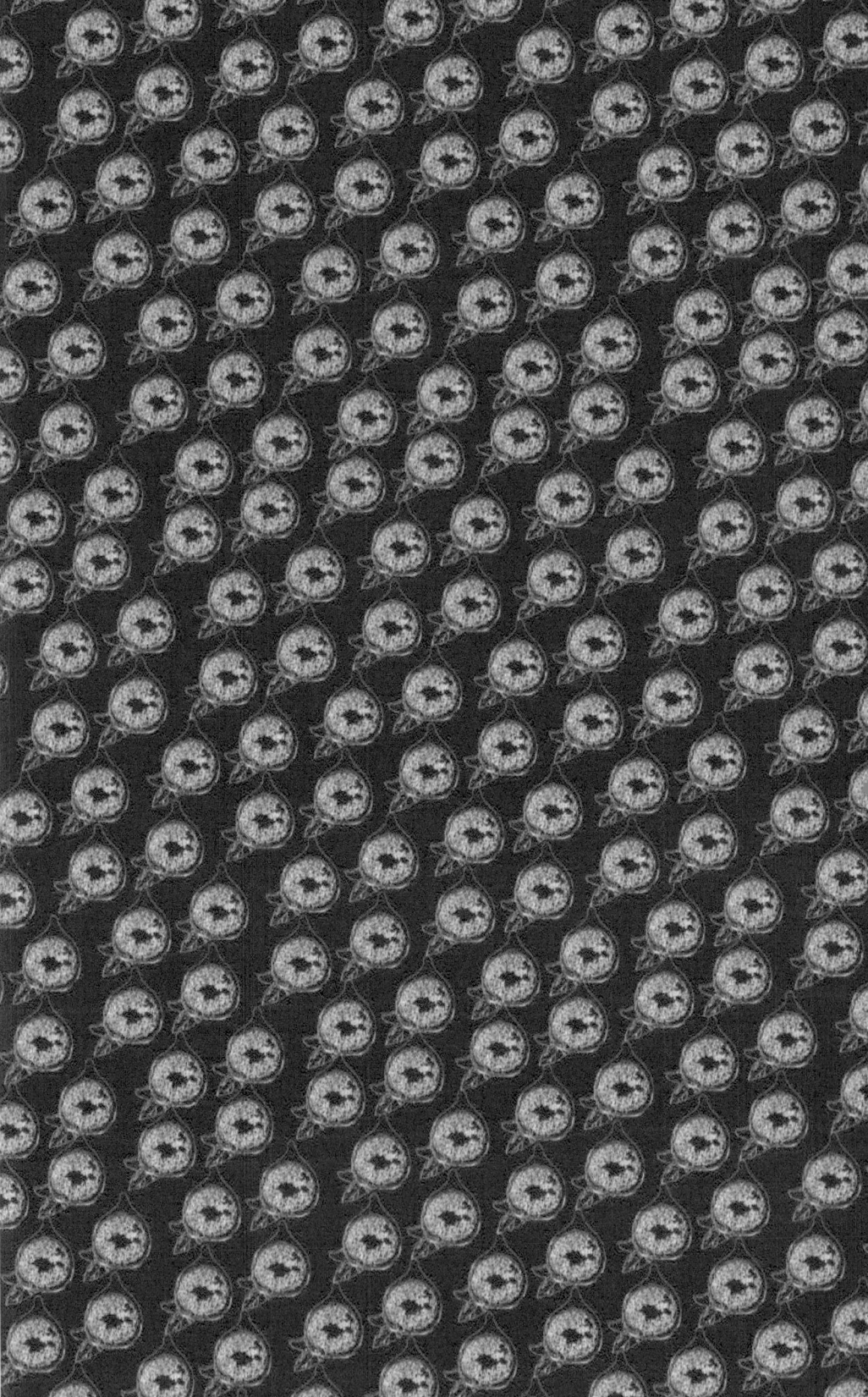

Special Thanks to
Everyone who supported me
this Inktober

Contact me:
littlebluejayboi@gmail.com
Tumblr
Instagram

*The genders of
the characters in this zine
are completely up to
interpretation*

*All Characters are at least
Eighteen years of age*

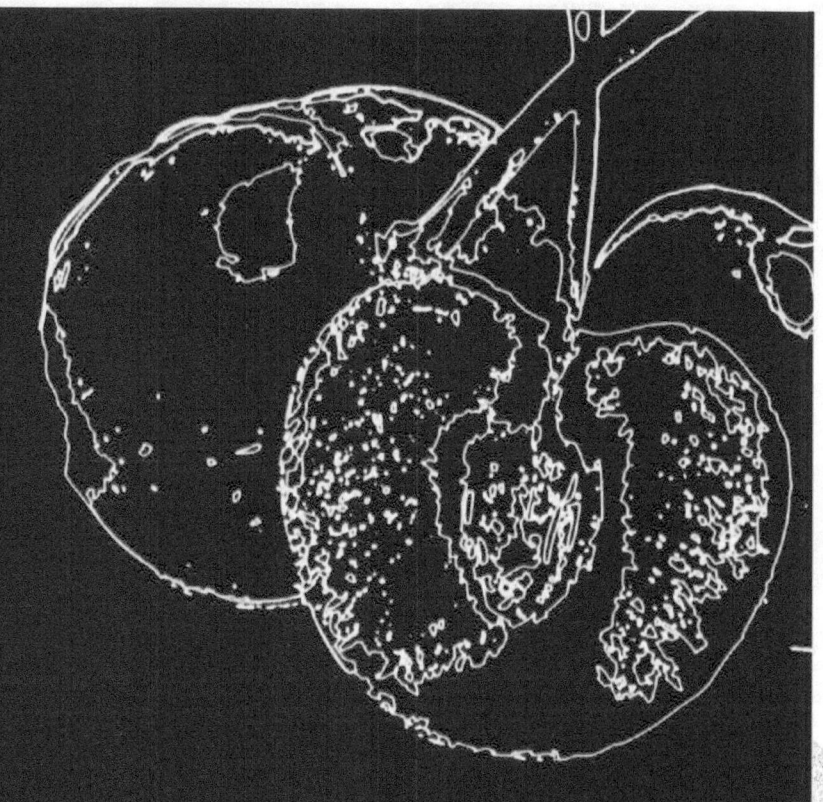

And even if I tasted
the sweetest nectar
of the forbidden fruit
nothing could compare
to the taste
of you

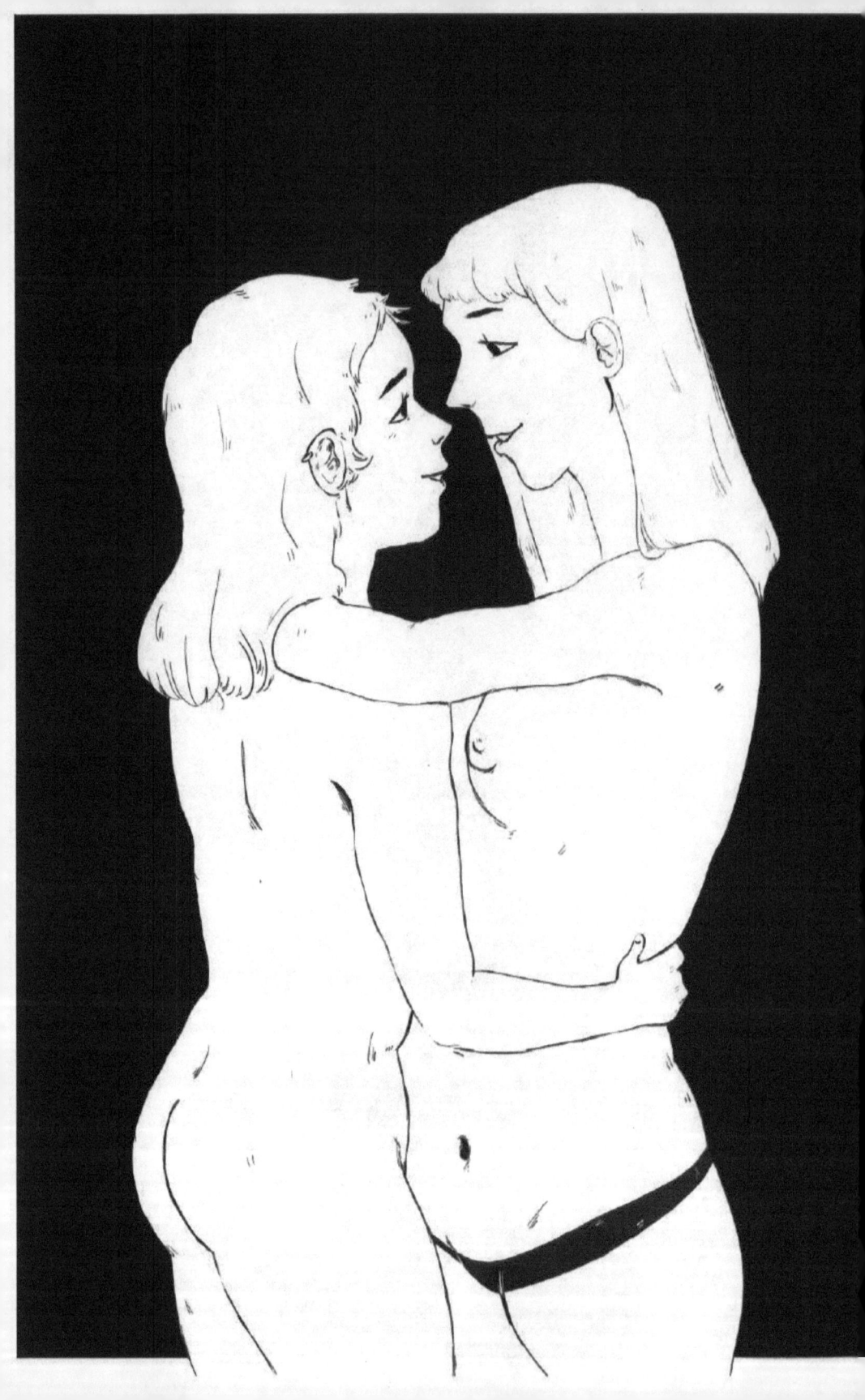

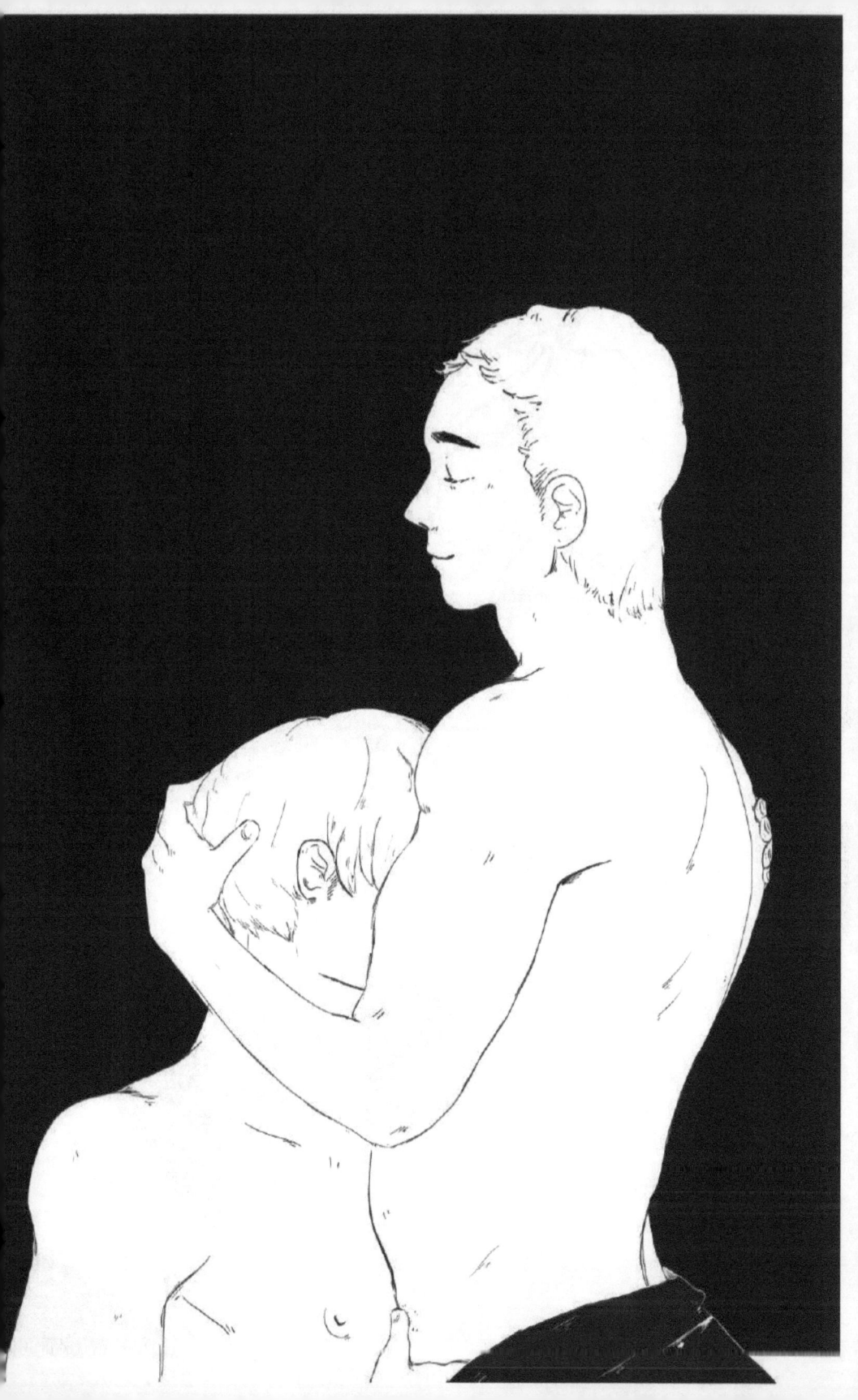

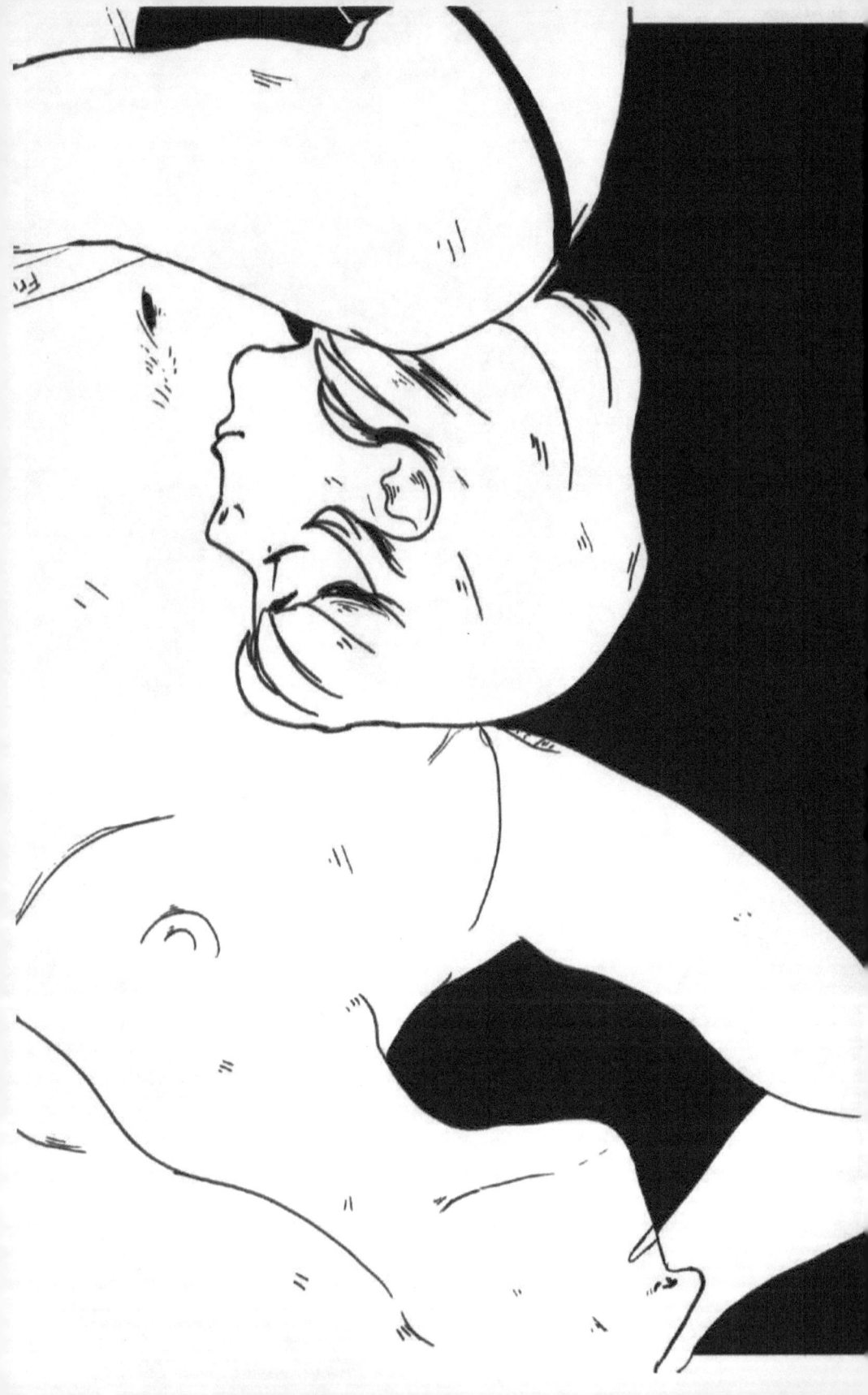

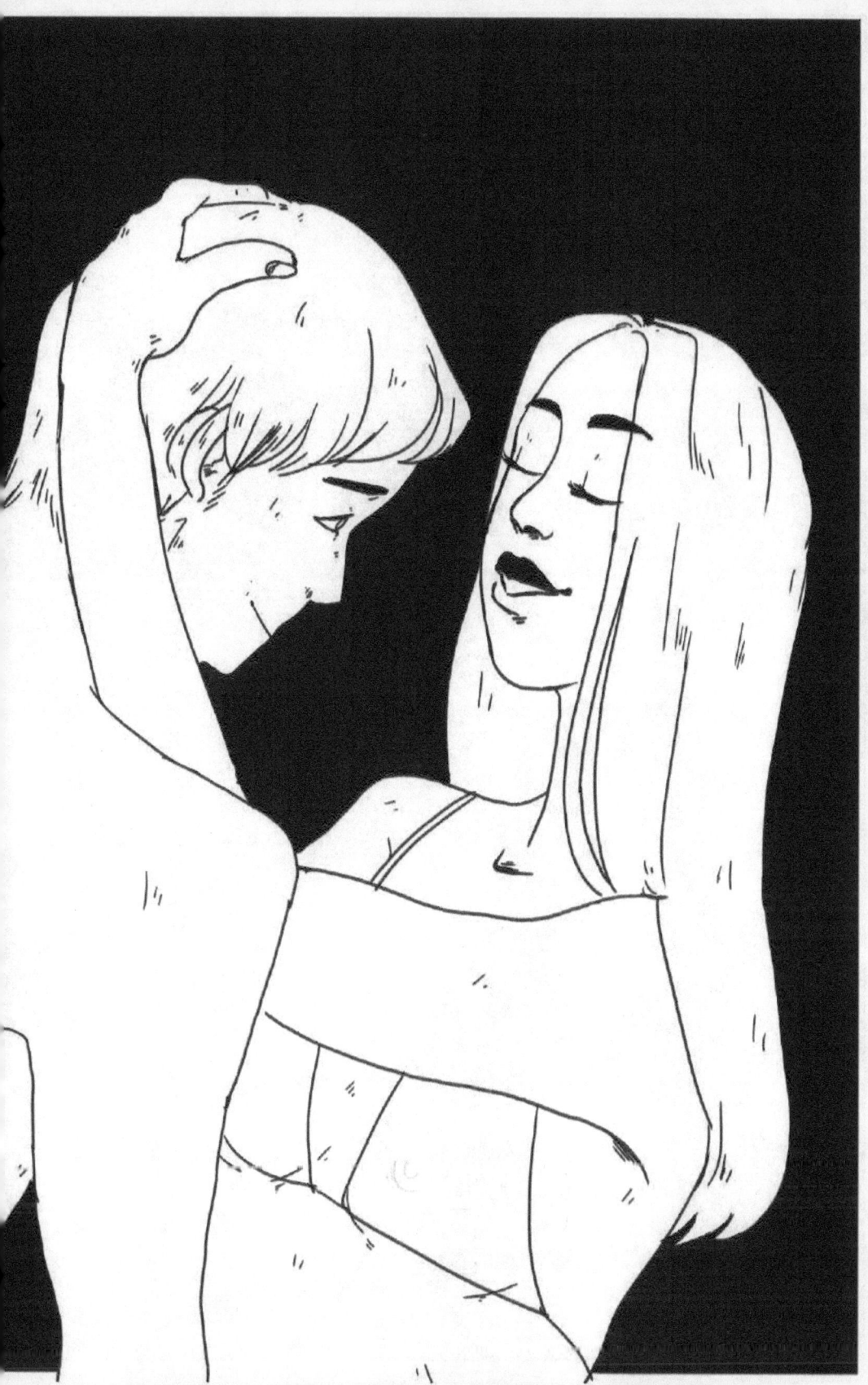

I looked into his eyes
and saw such fiery passion
then we kisssed
we cried
and
we lived.

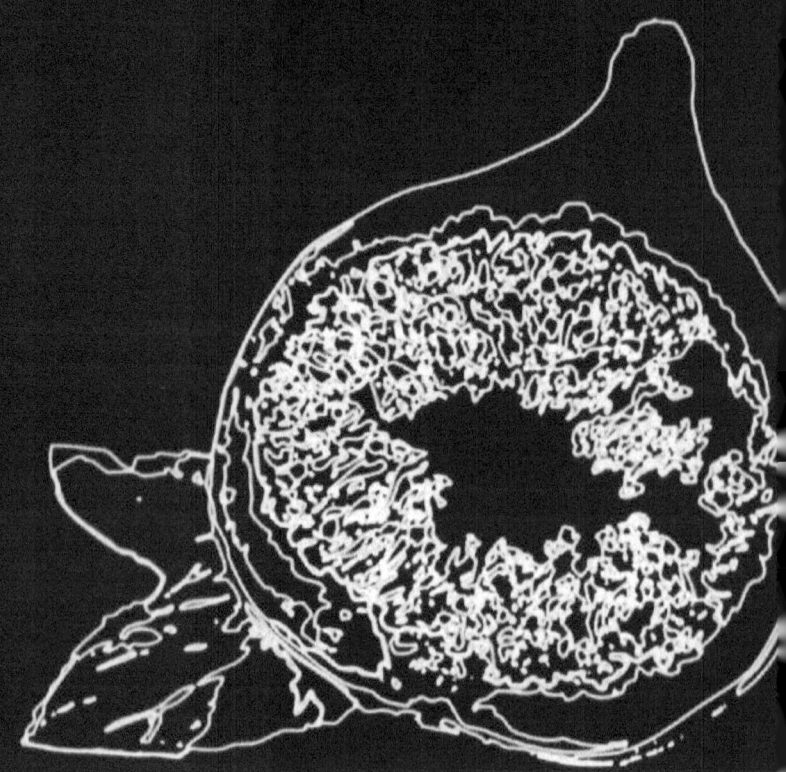

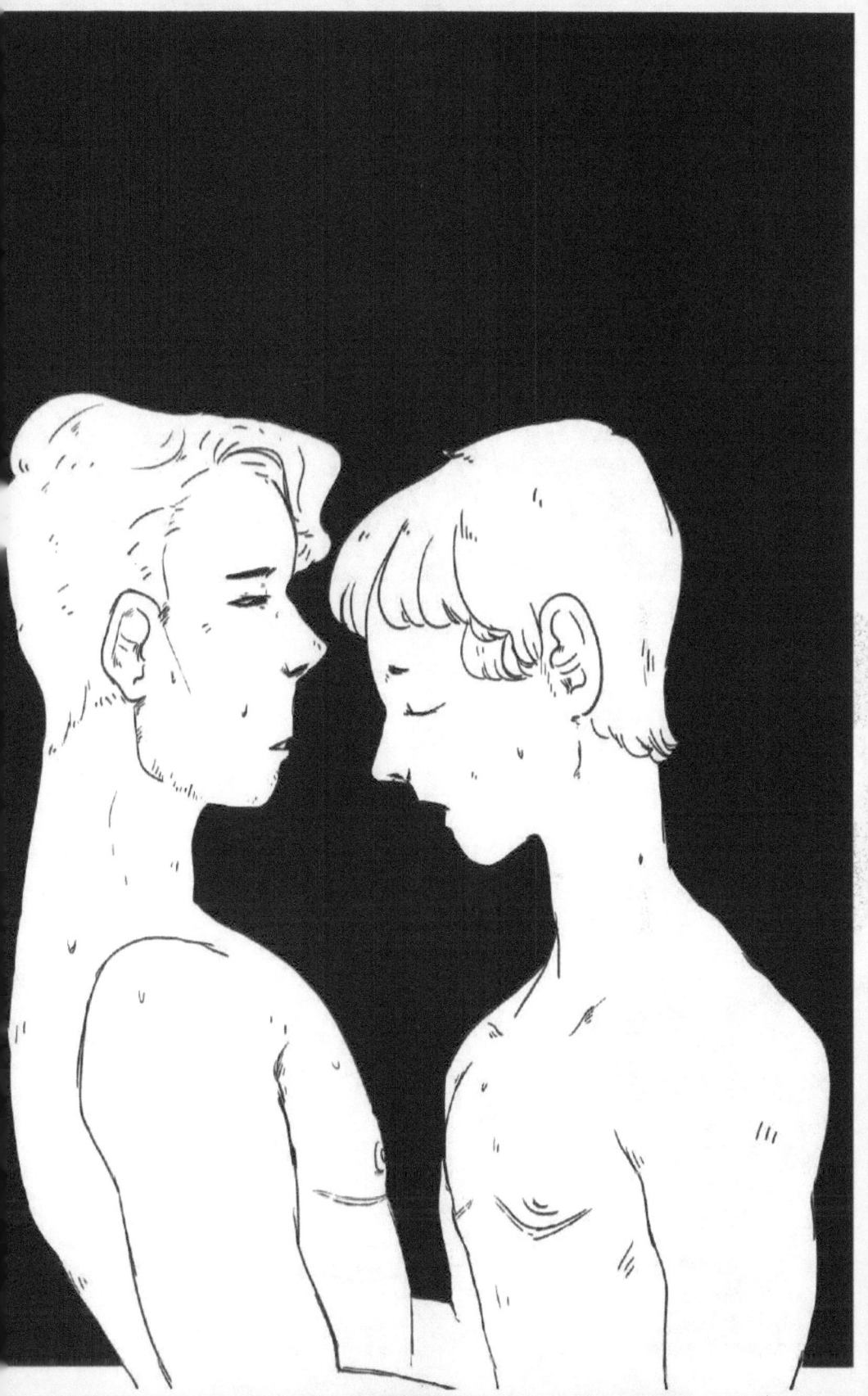

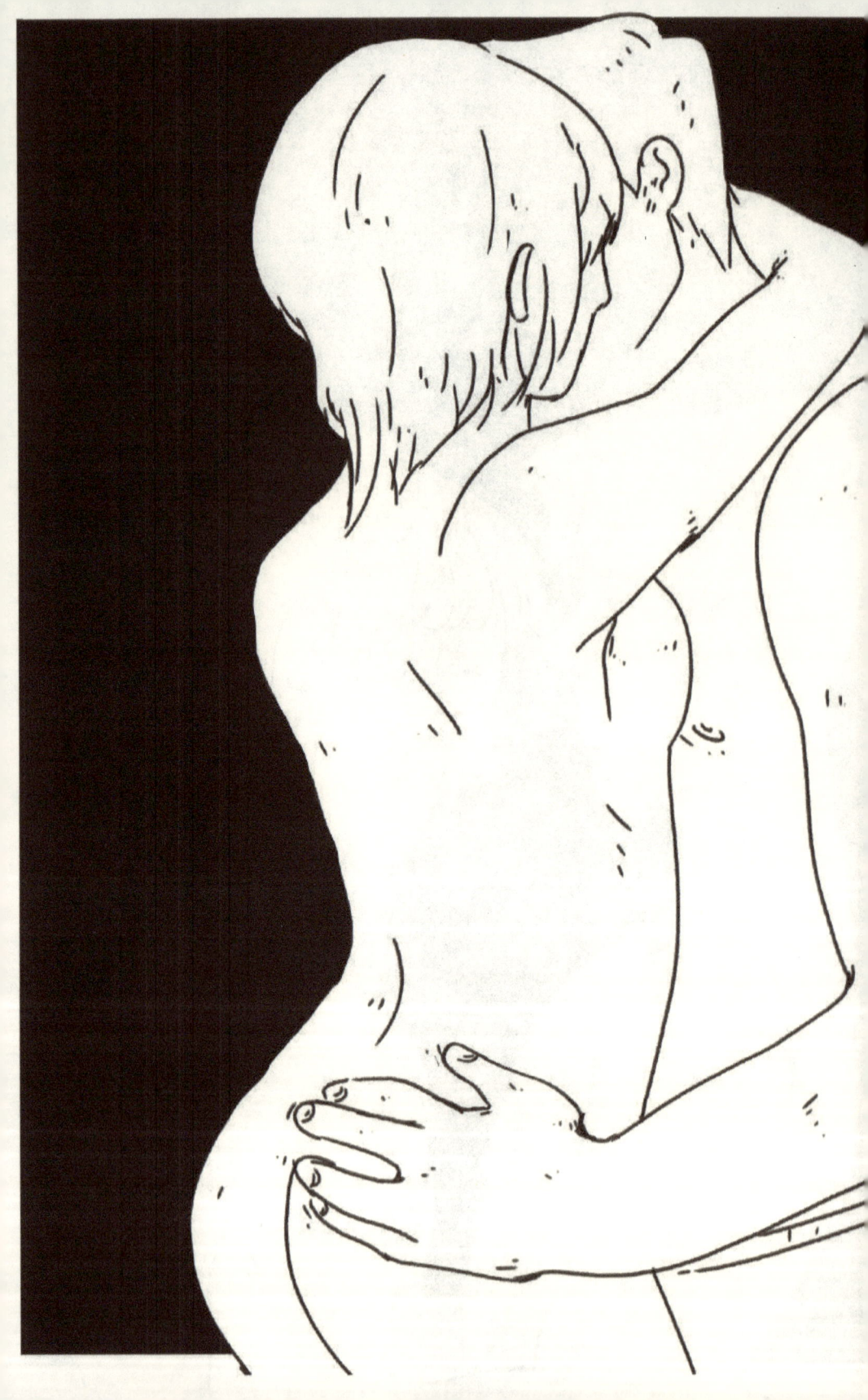

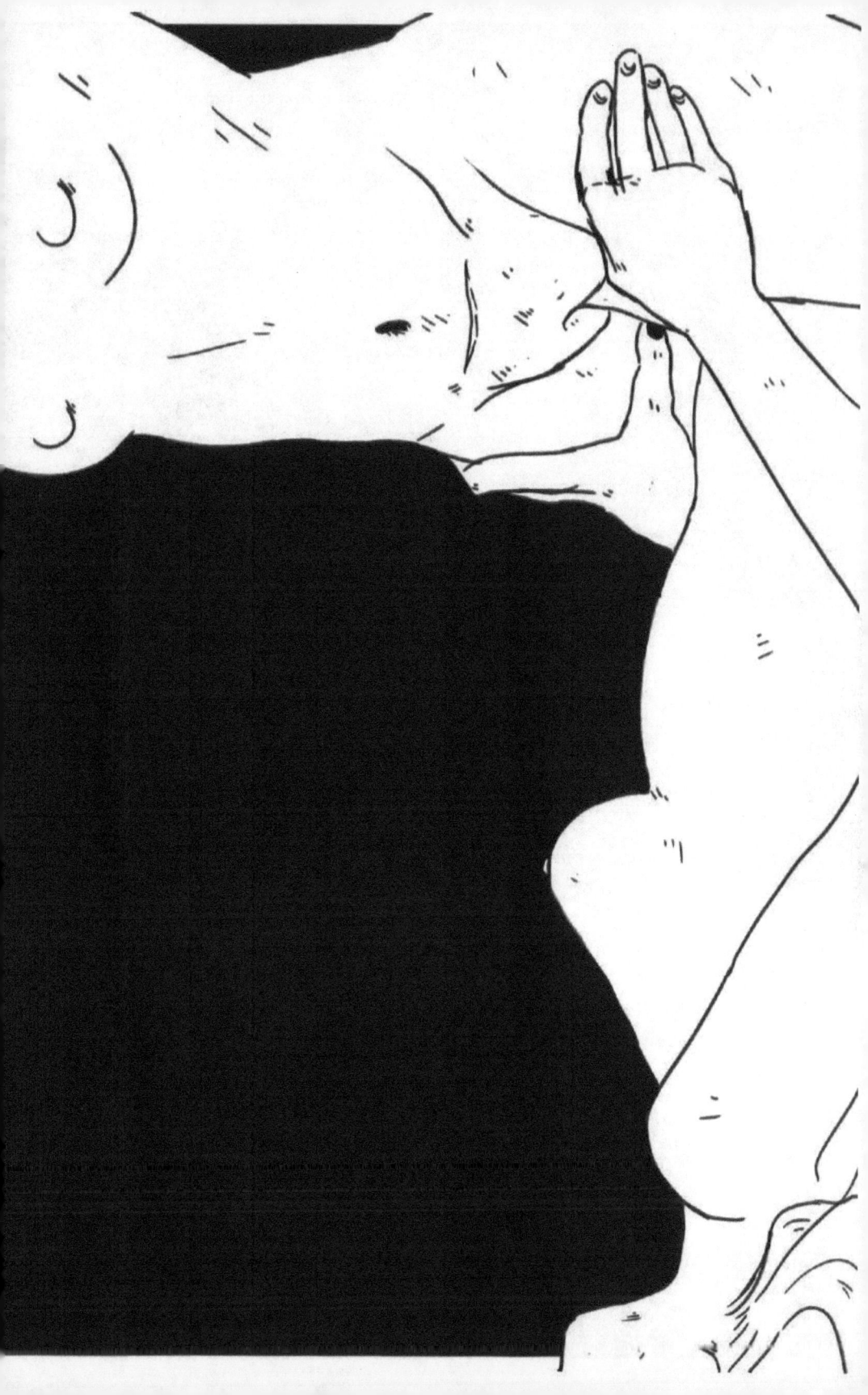

I sink my teeth into your
soft, pink skin—
chest ablaze with lust
only you could do this to me
only you could ever
drive me to the extreme

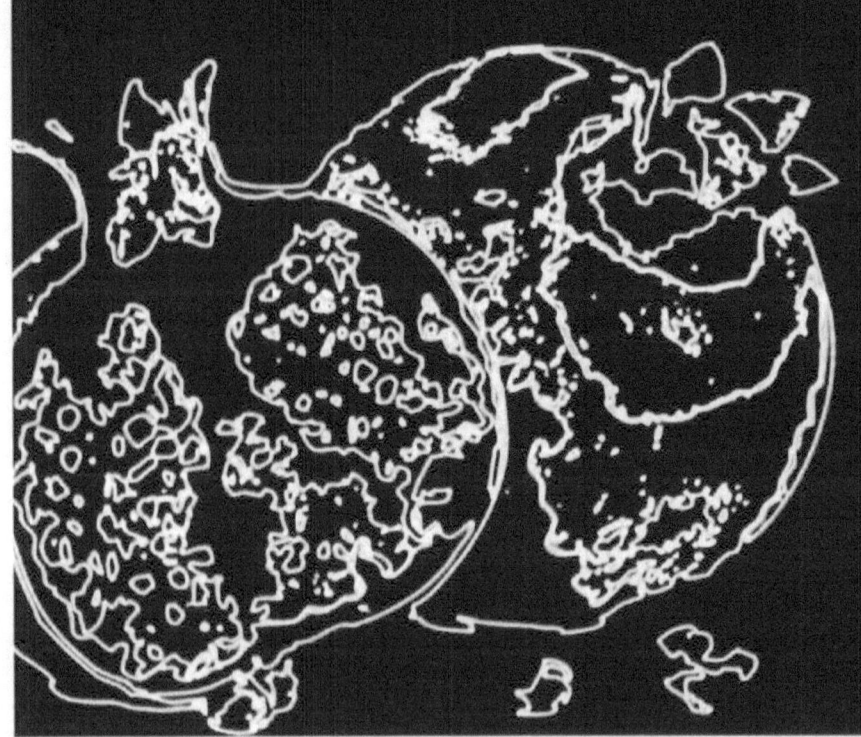

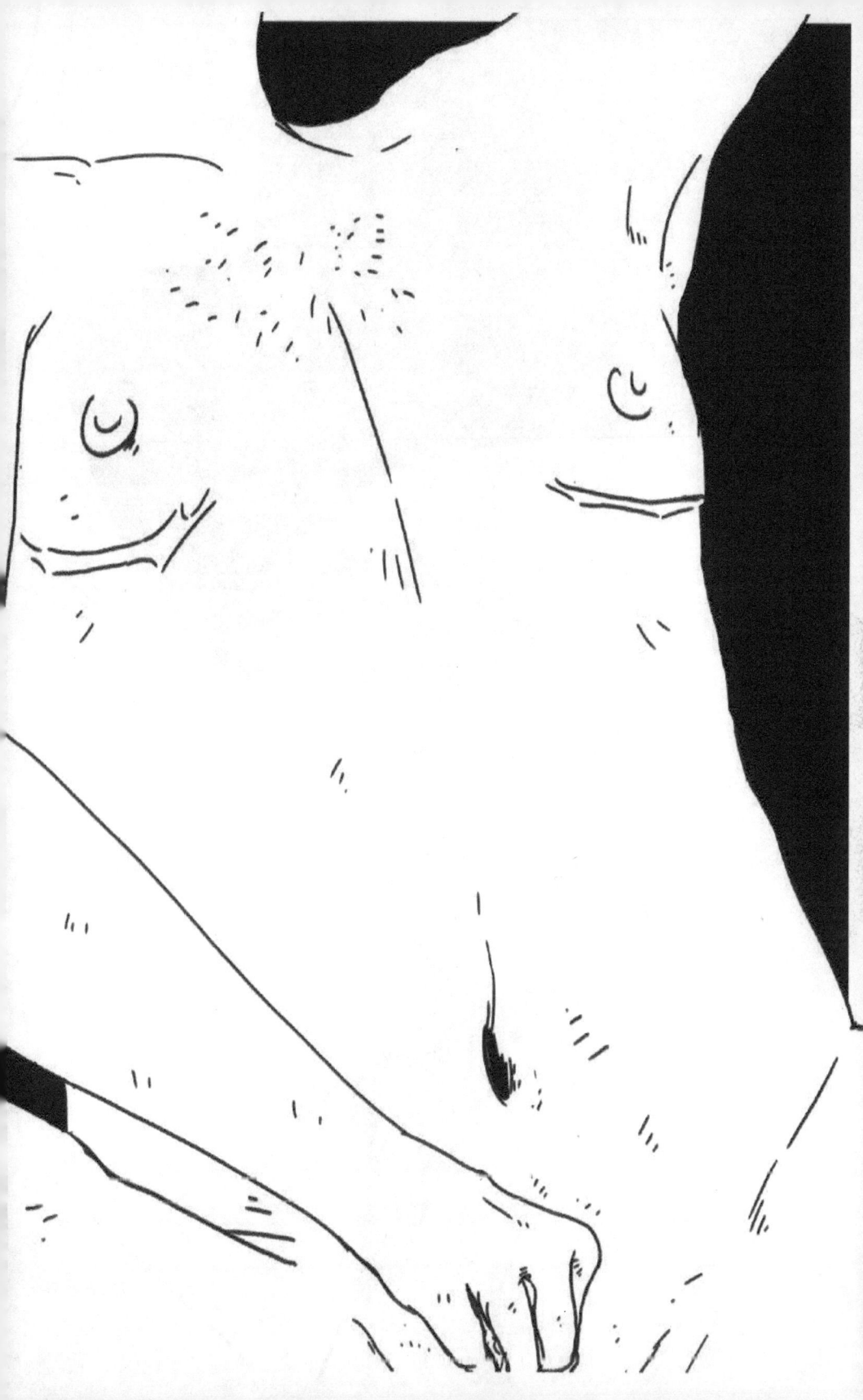

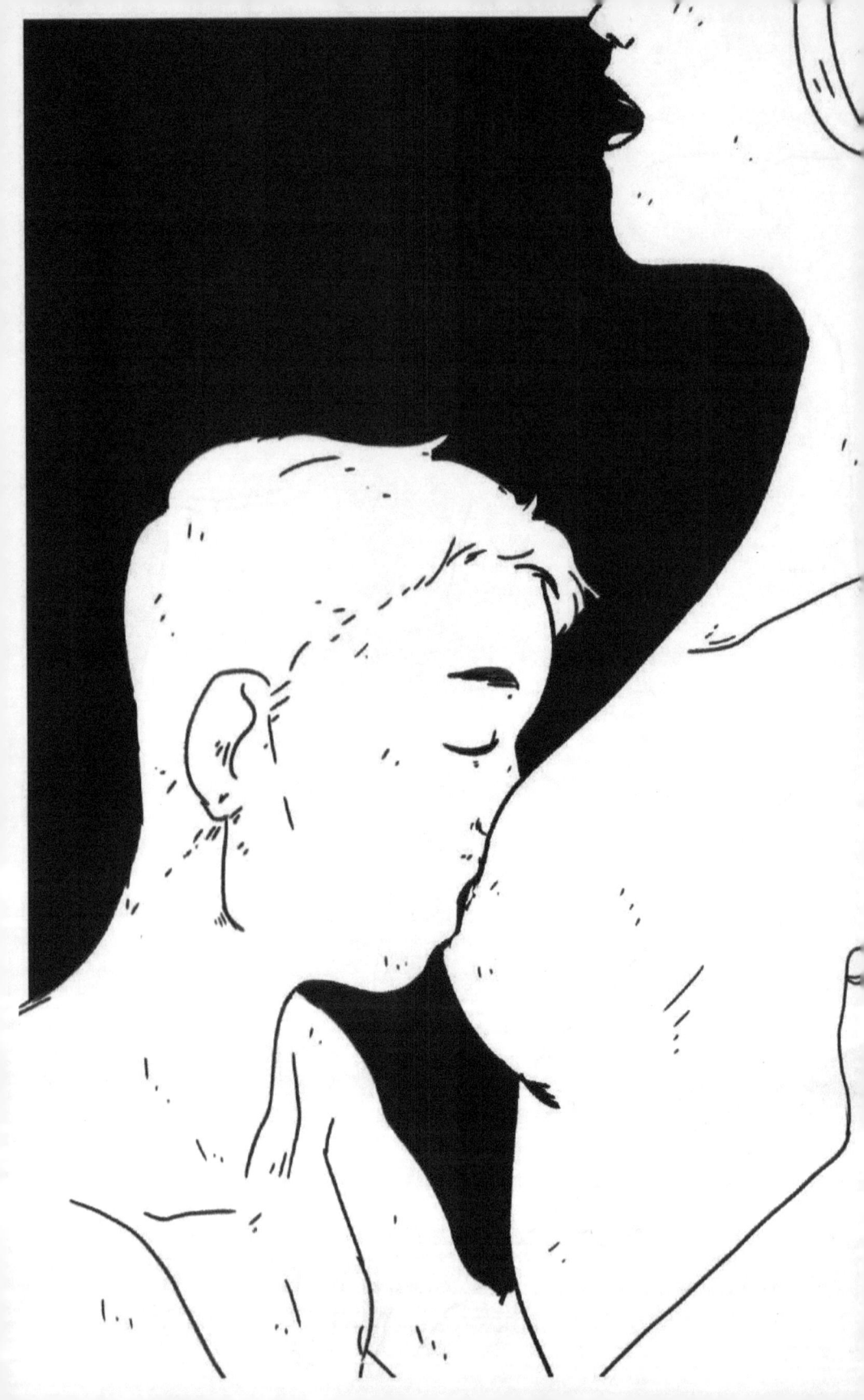

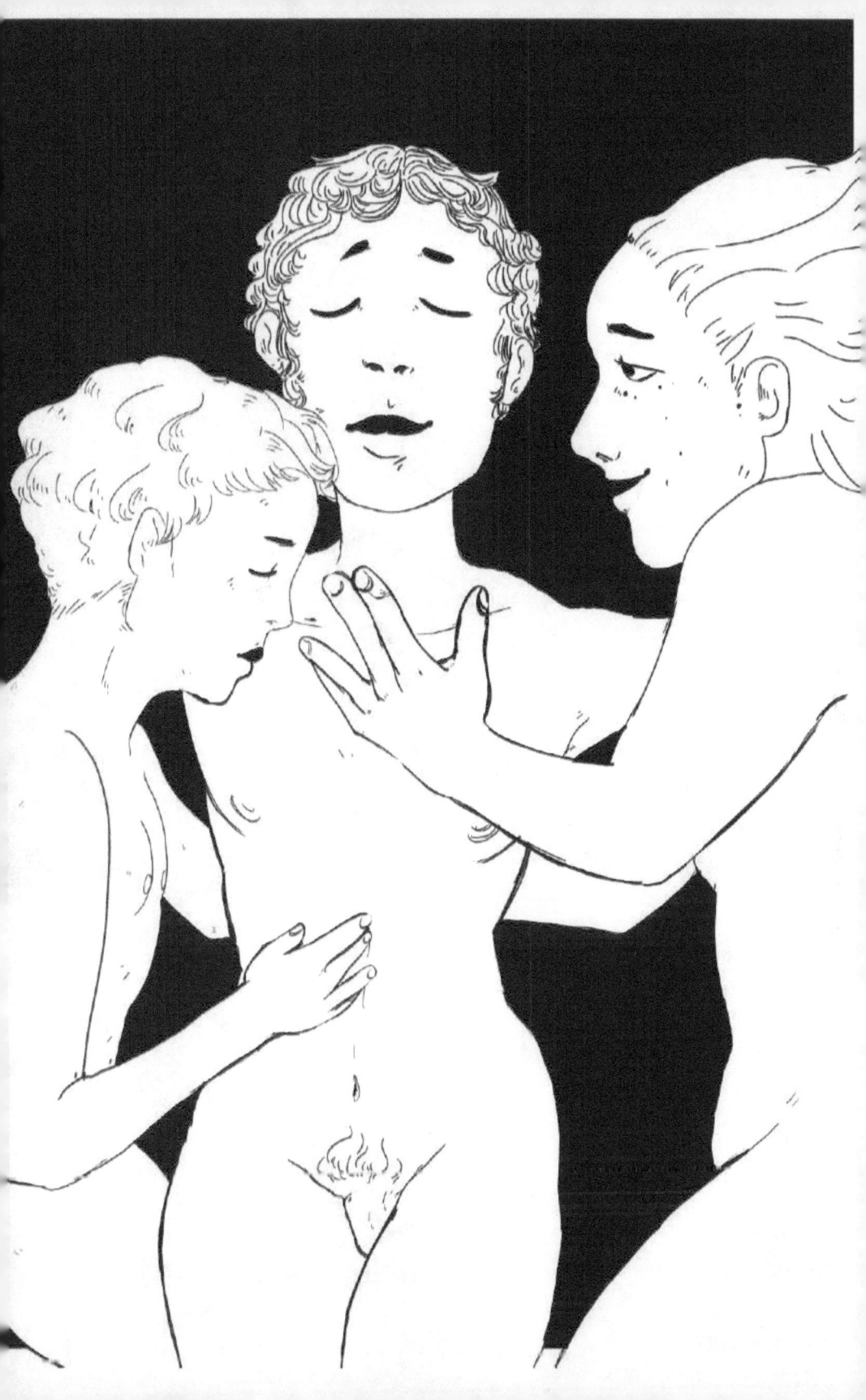

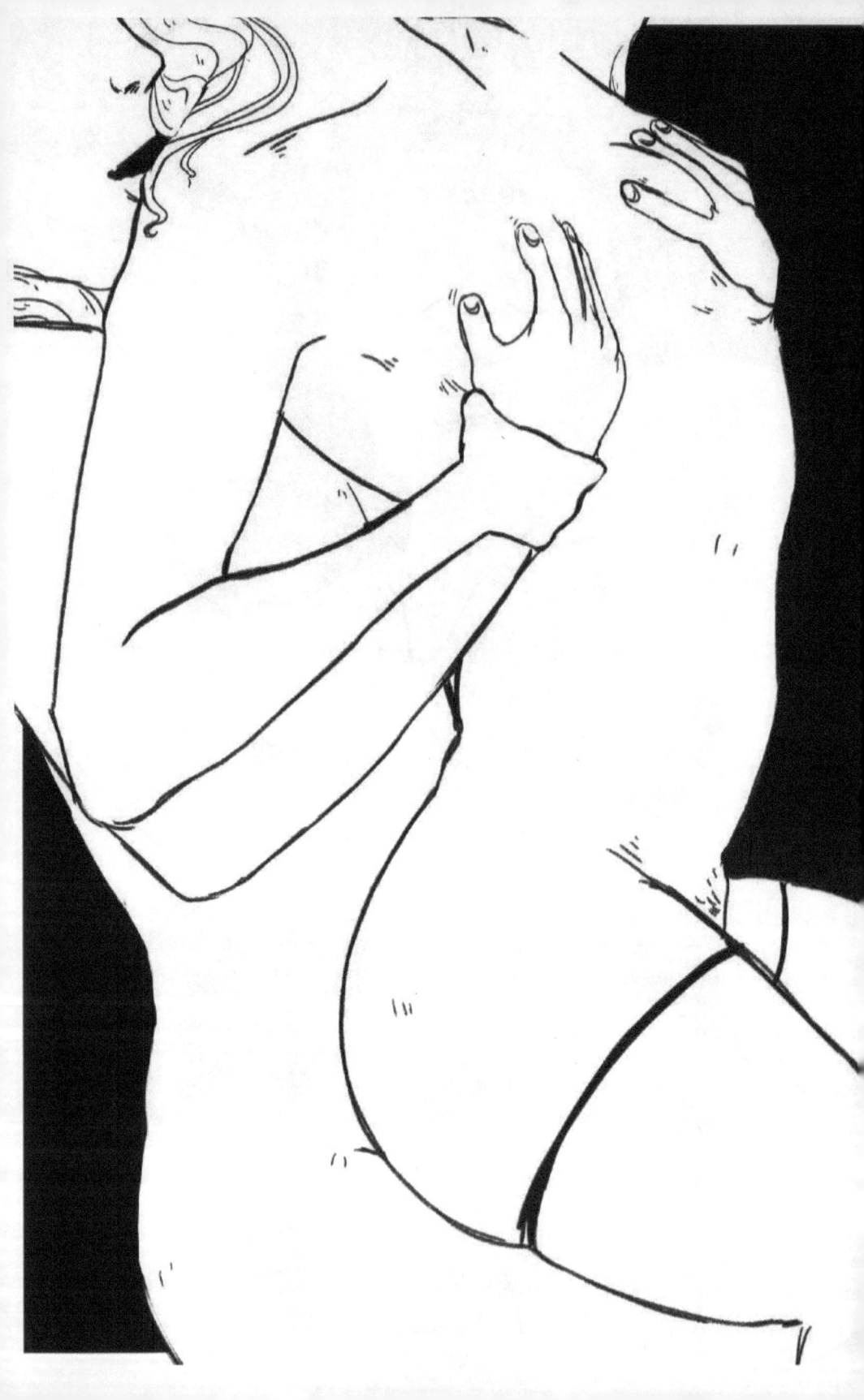

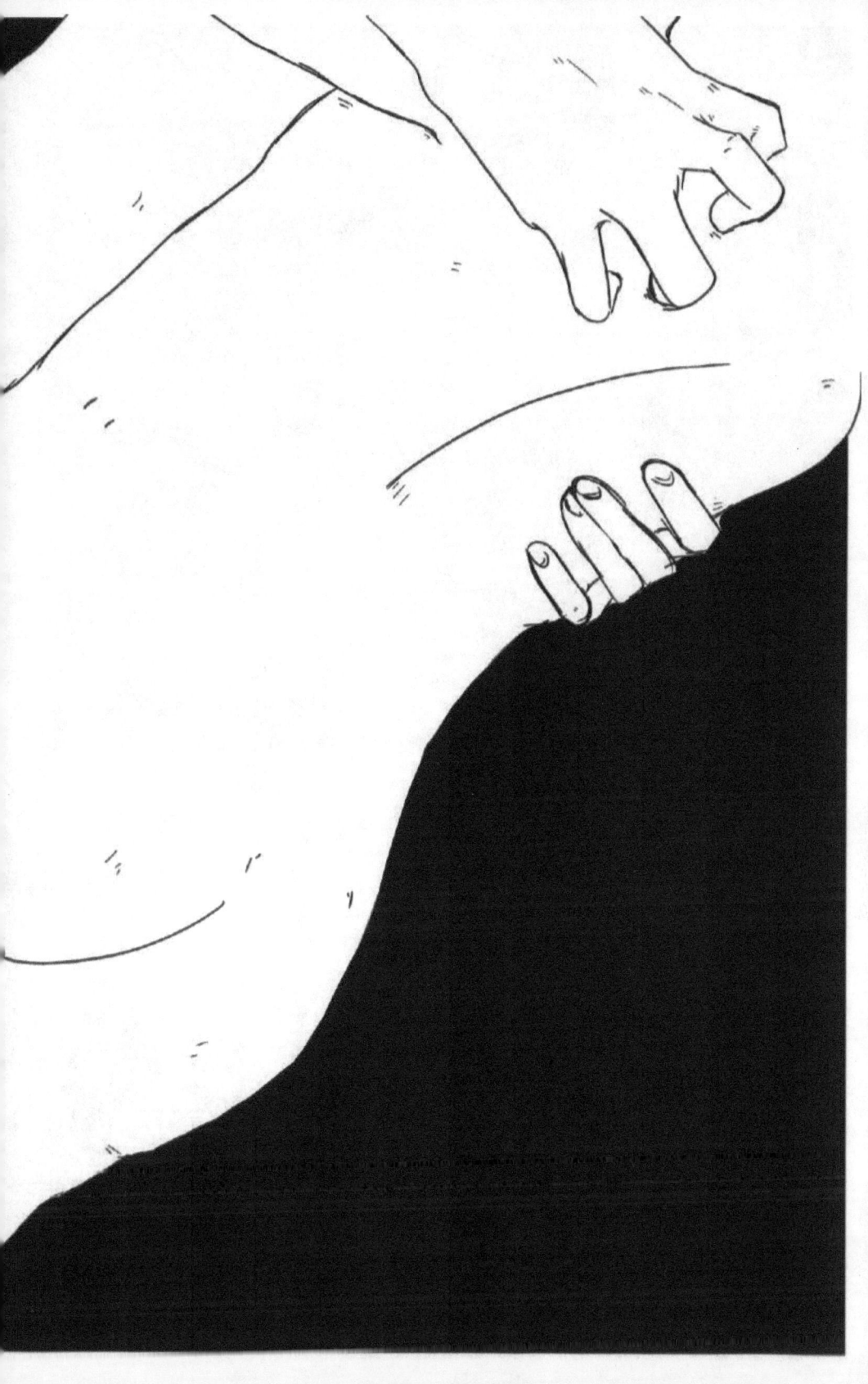

*If I loved myself
half as much as I loved you
I'd be as bad
as Narcissus himself.*

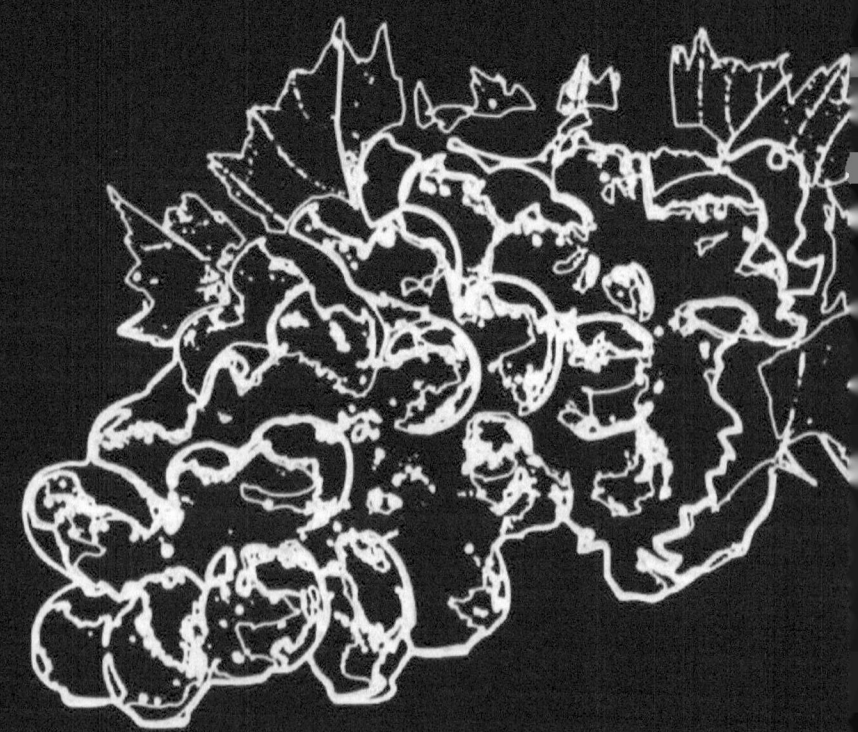

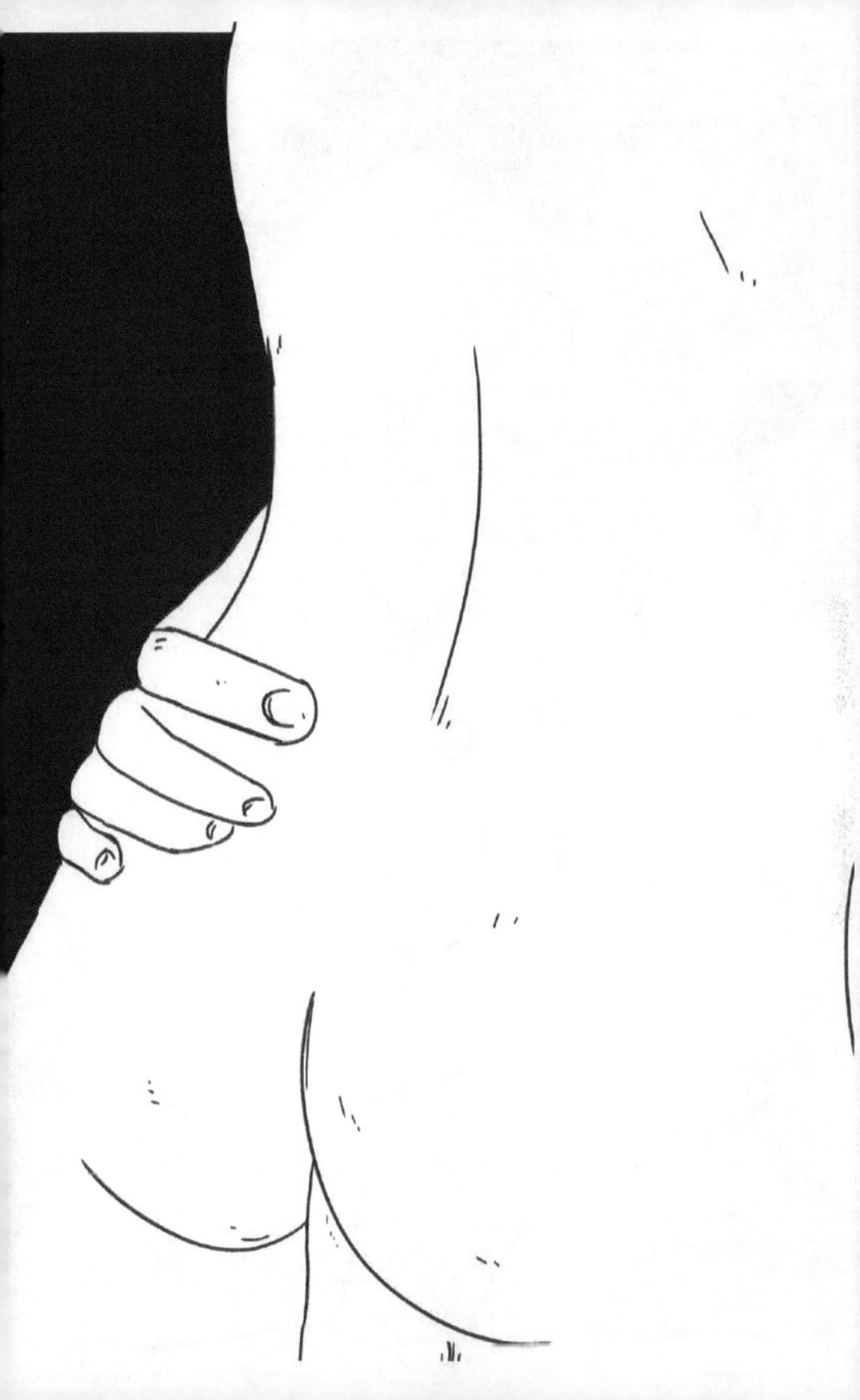

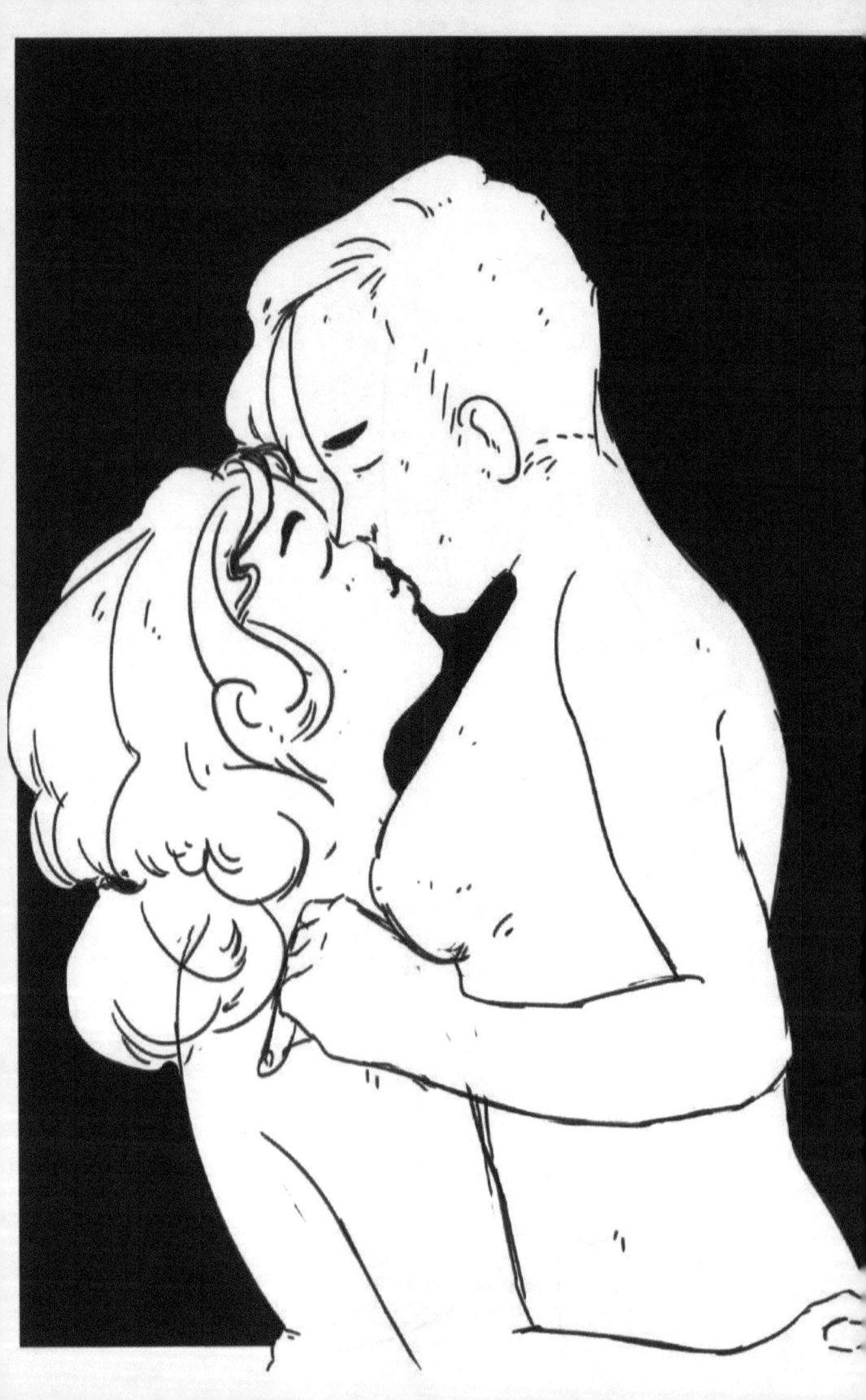

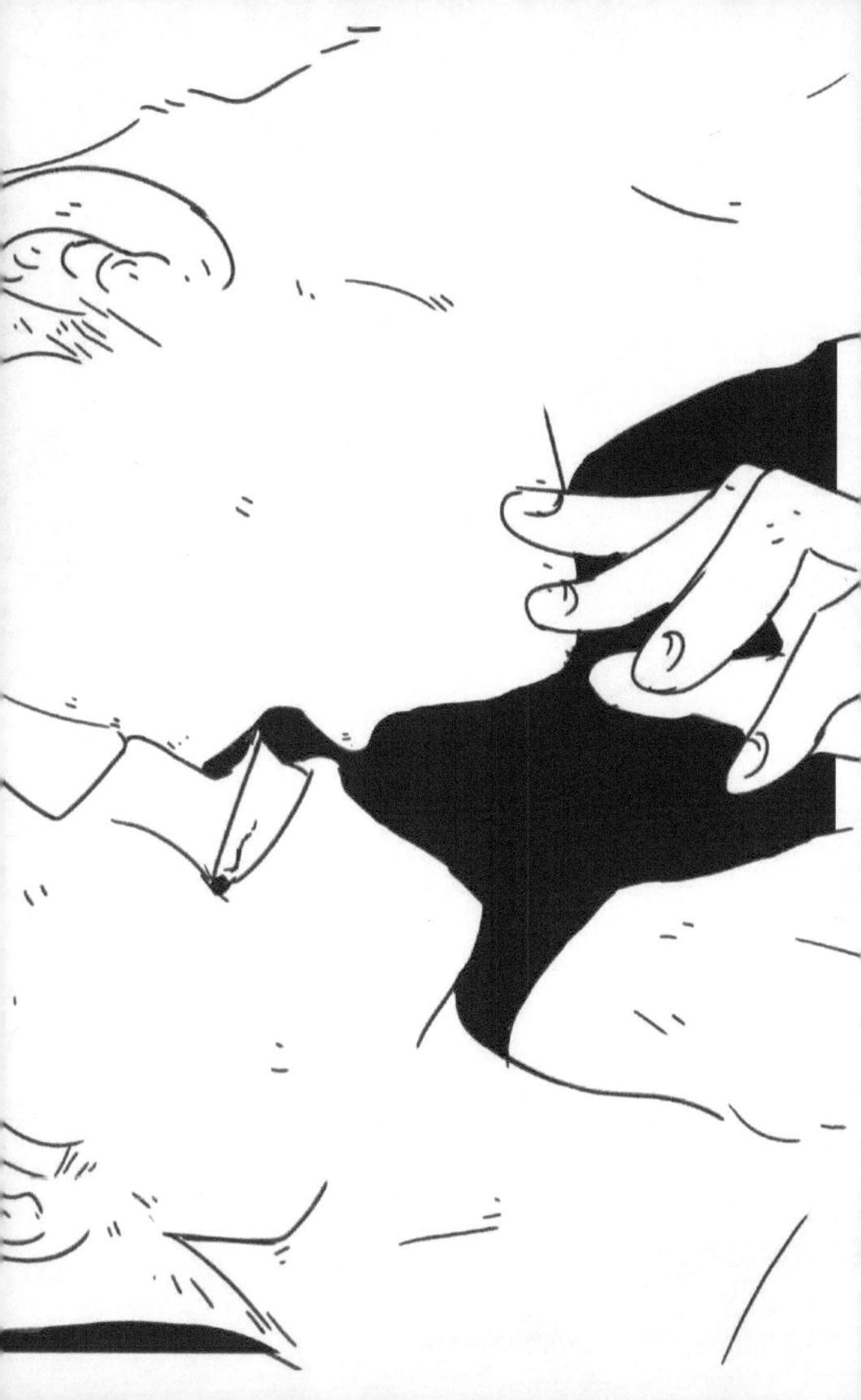

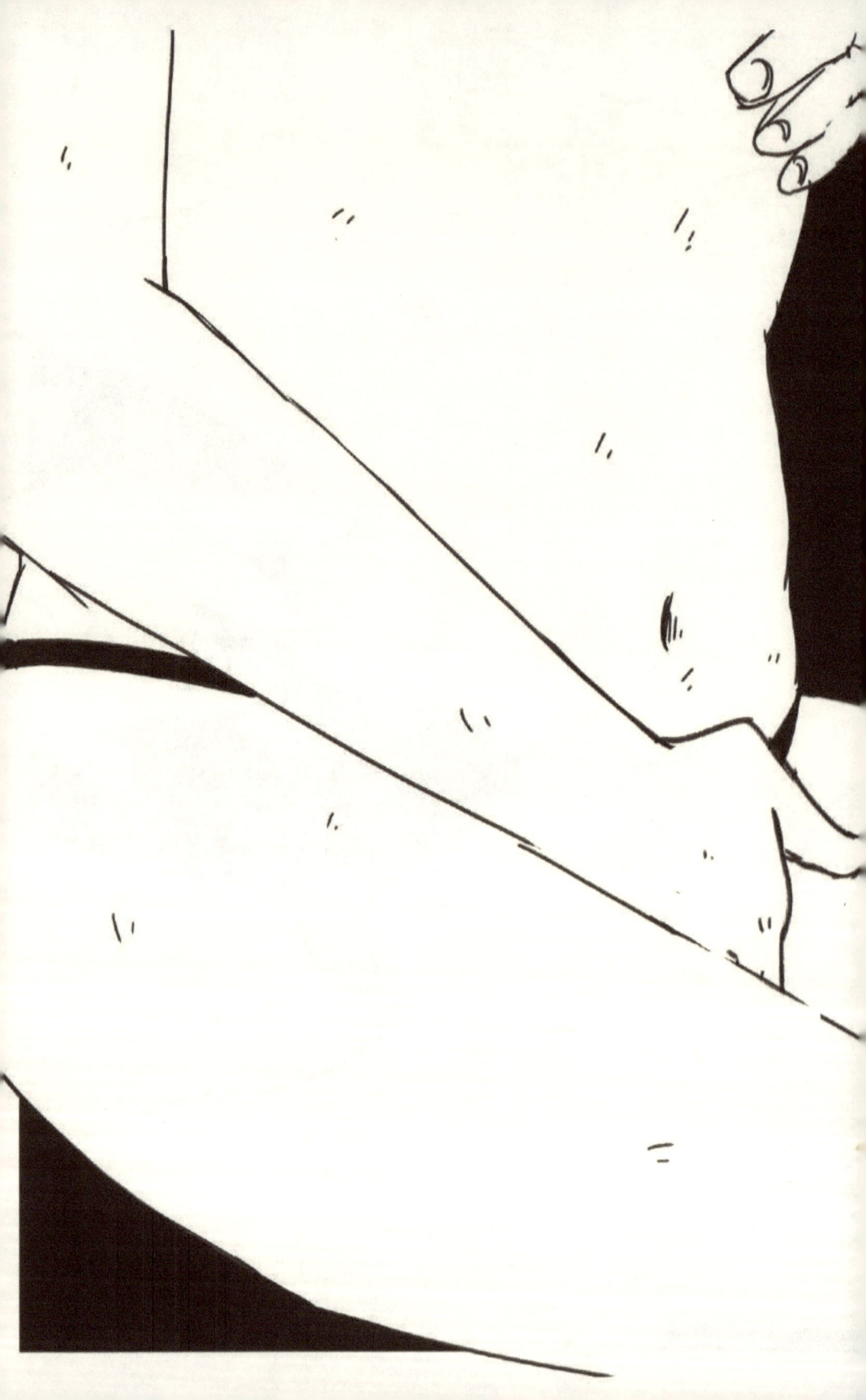

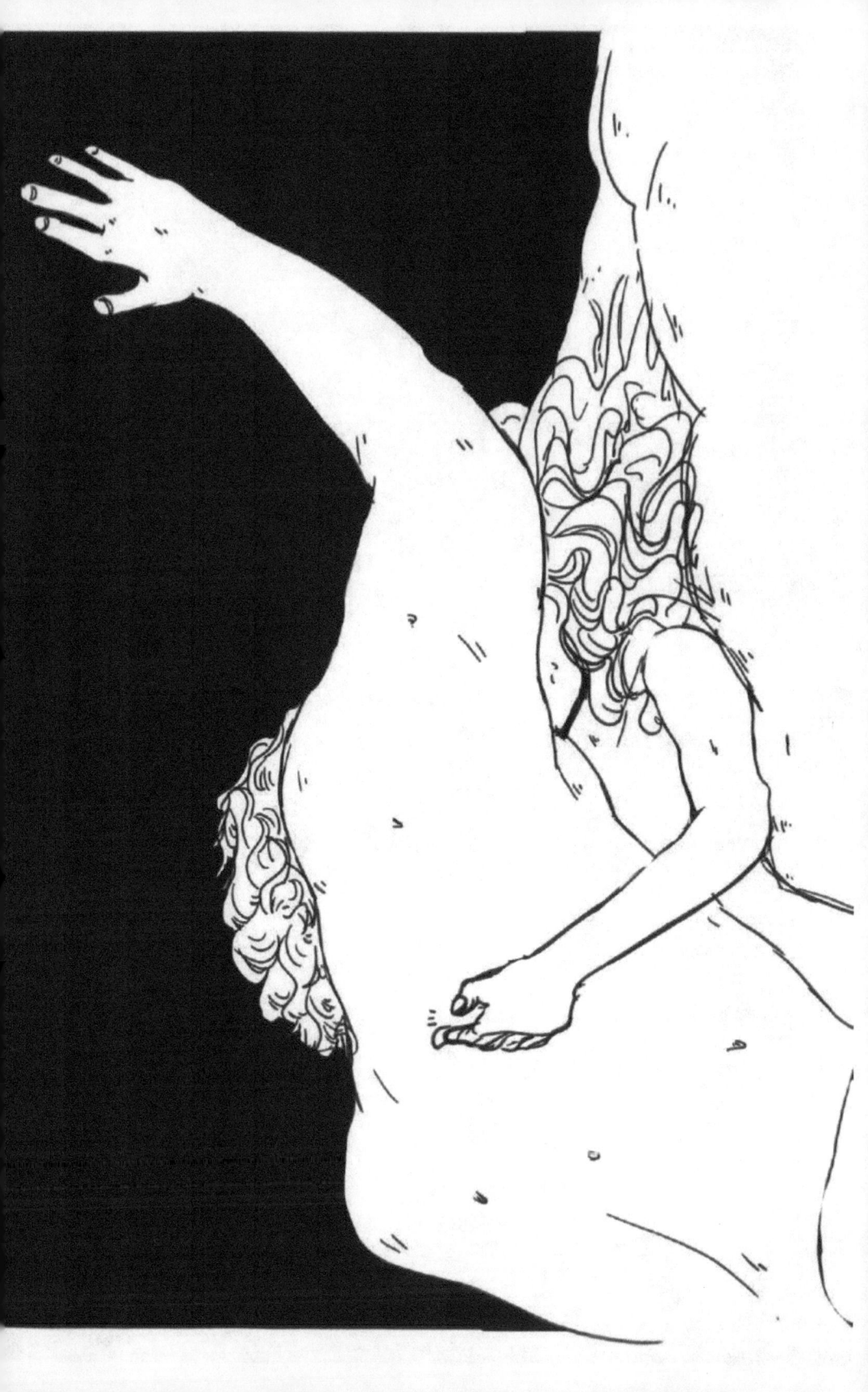

*Like the sweetest peach
she was ripe for the picking
and I took her hand
and ate her right up*

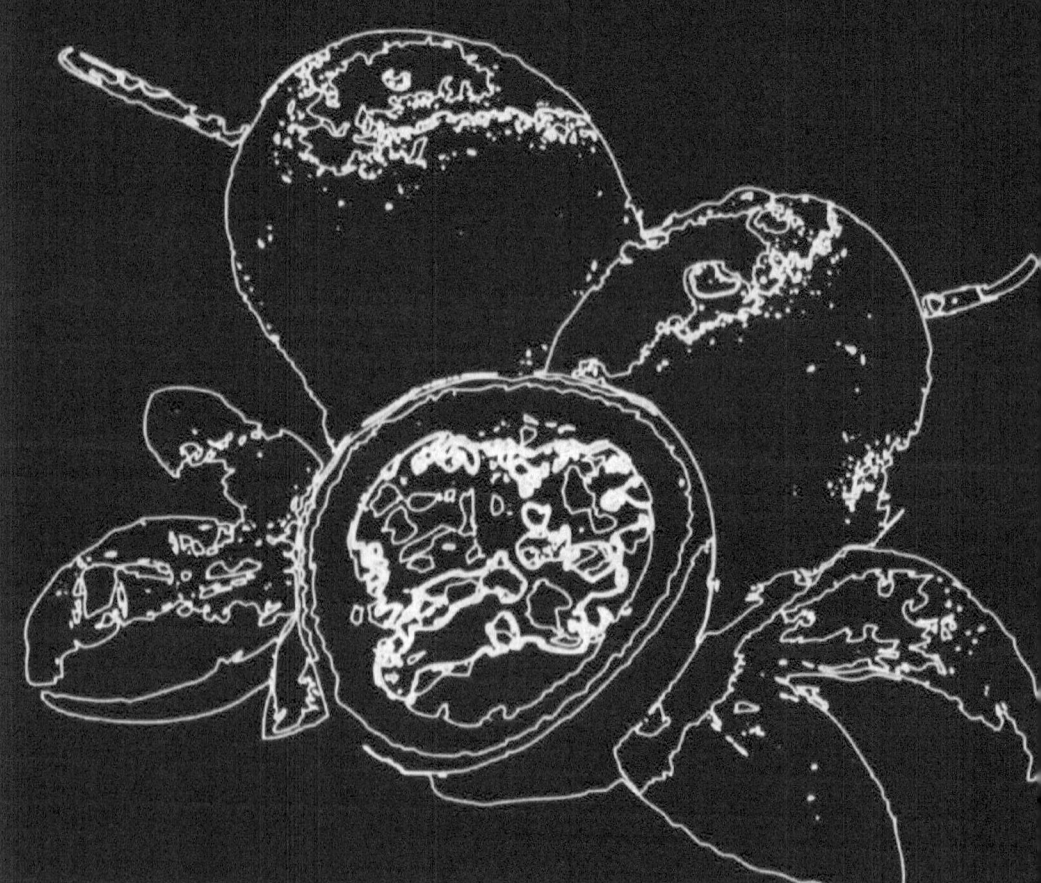

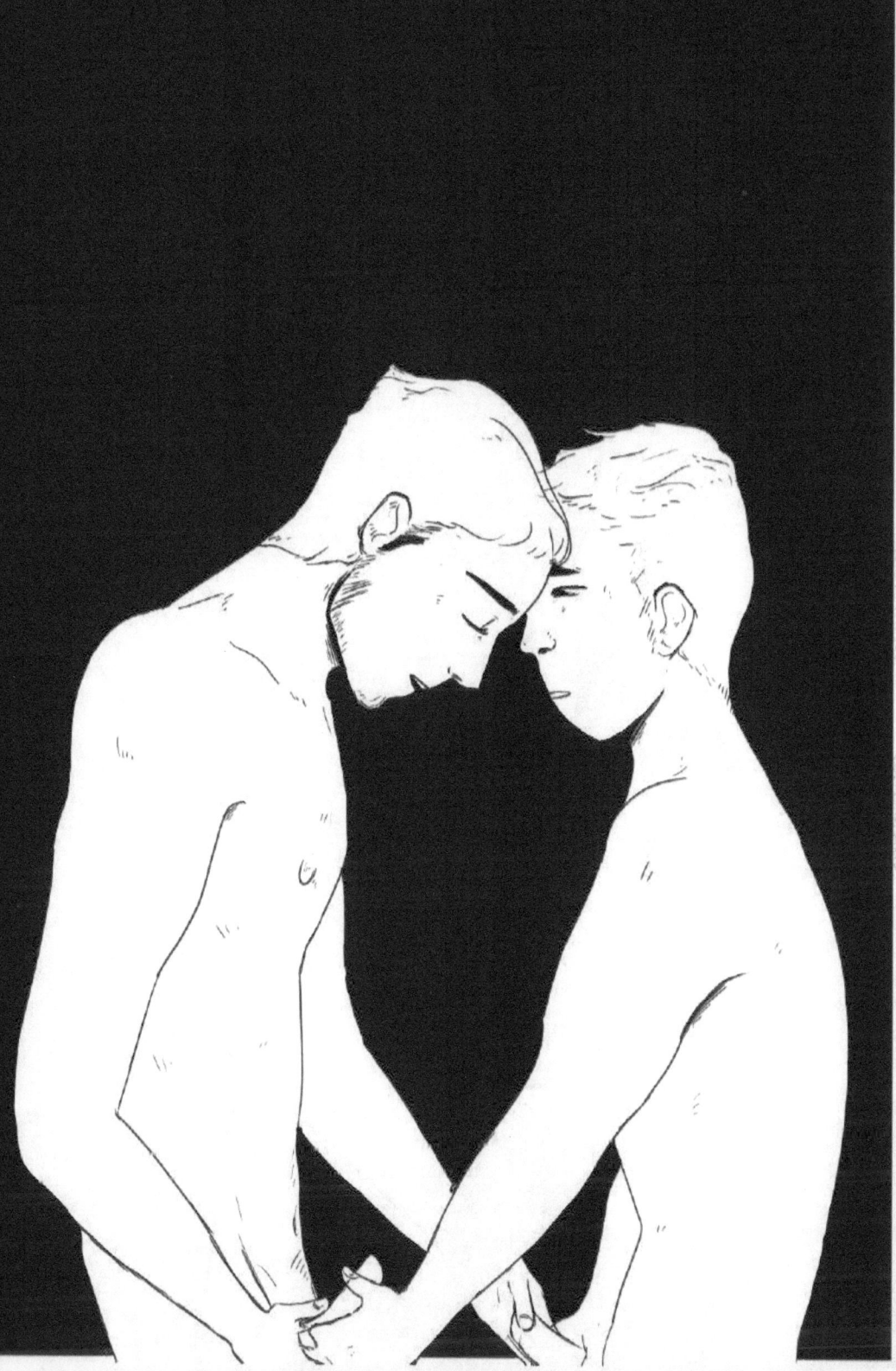

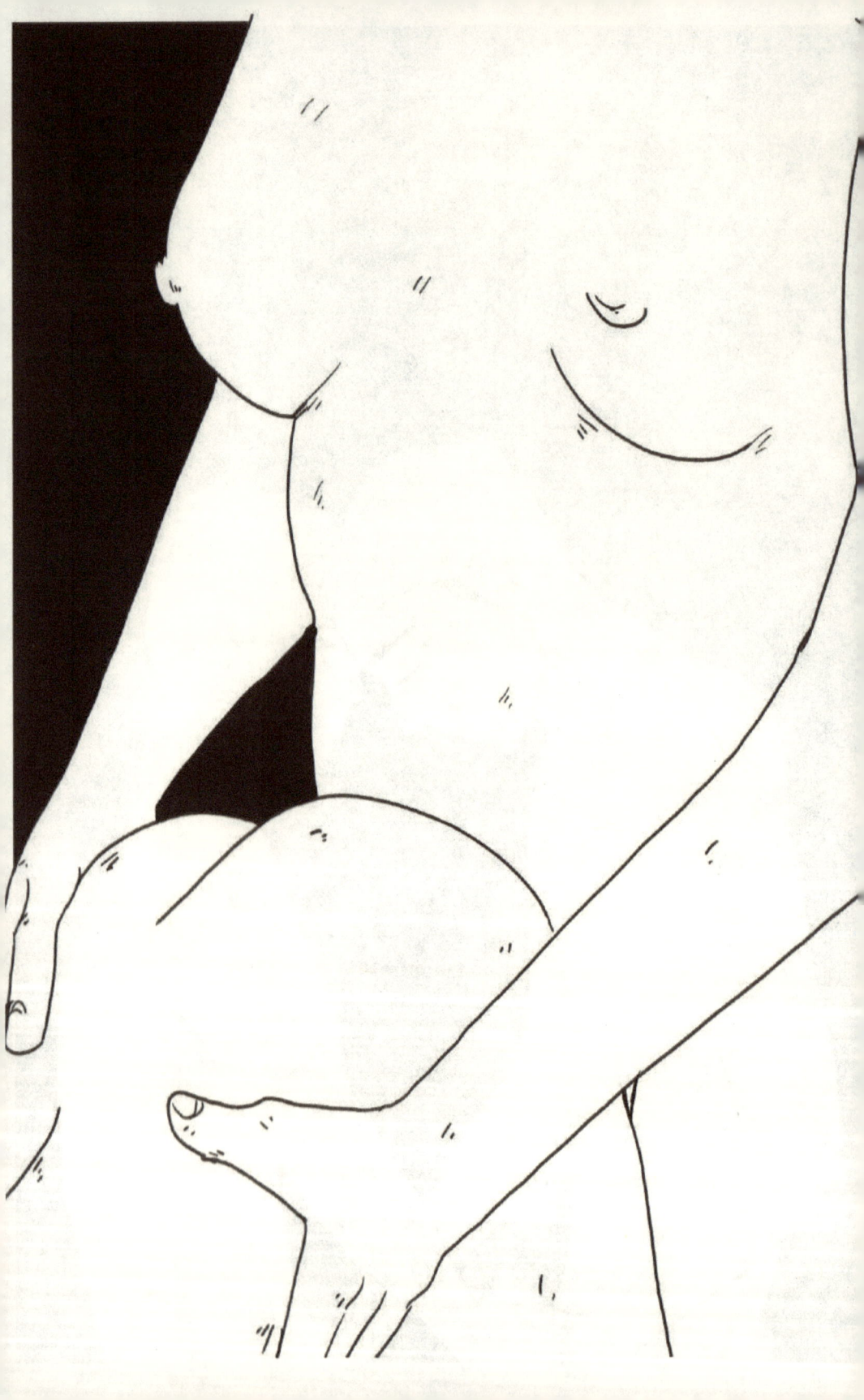

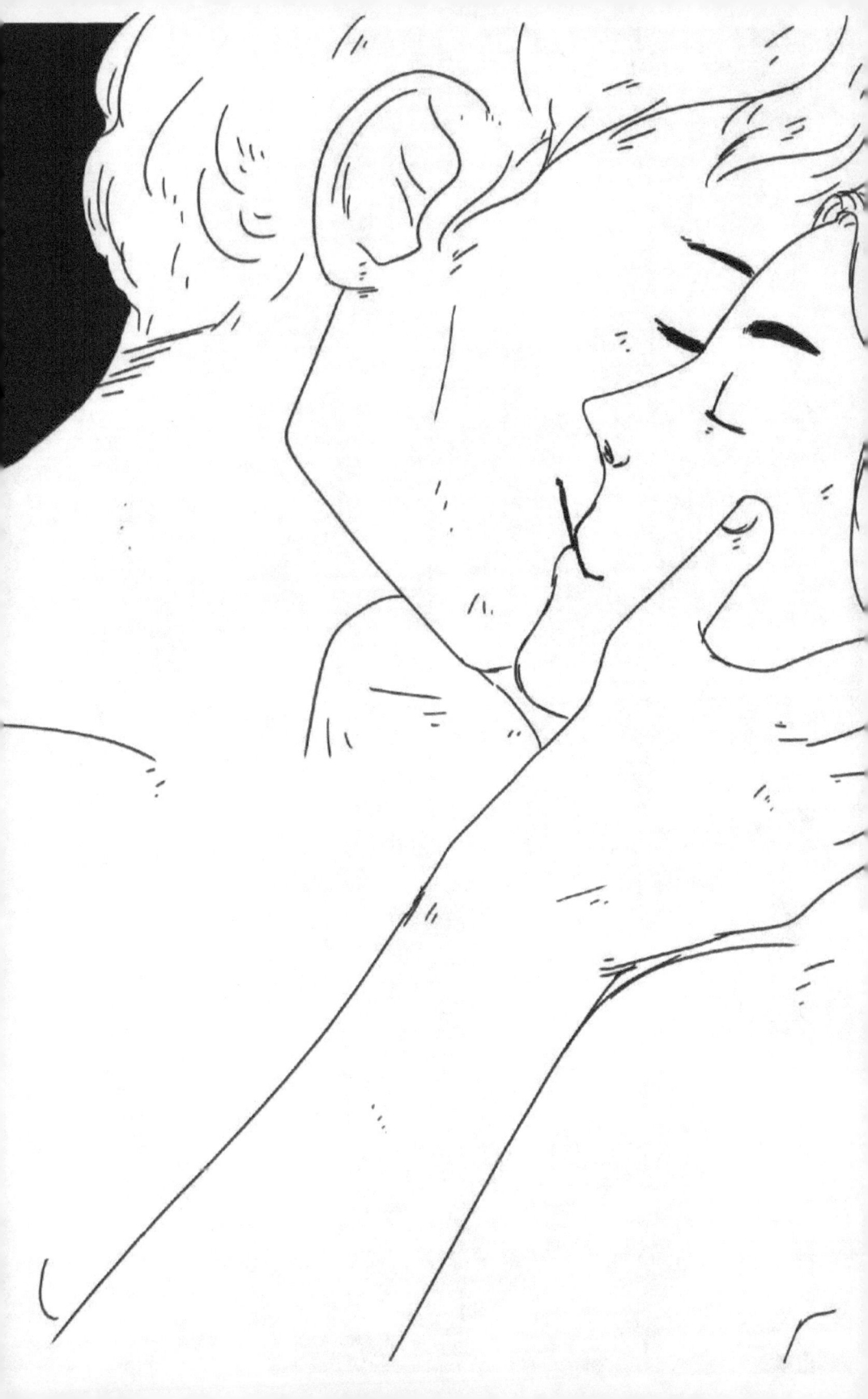

*His hand took mine
and it was like the whole world
was suddenly at our mercy.
We were powerful, passionate
and so utterly in love
that I can't even begin
to describe it.*

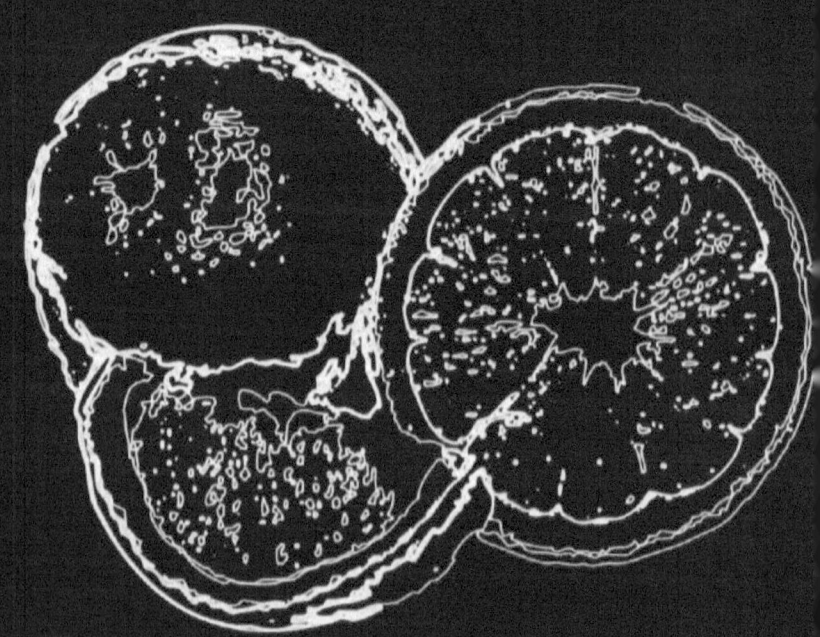

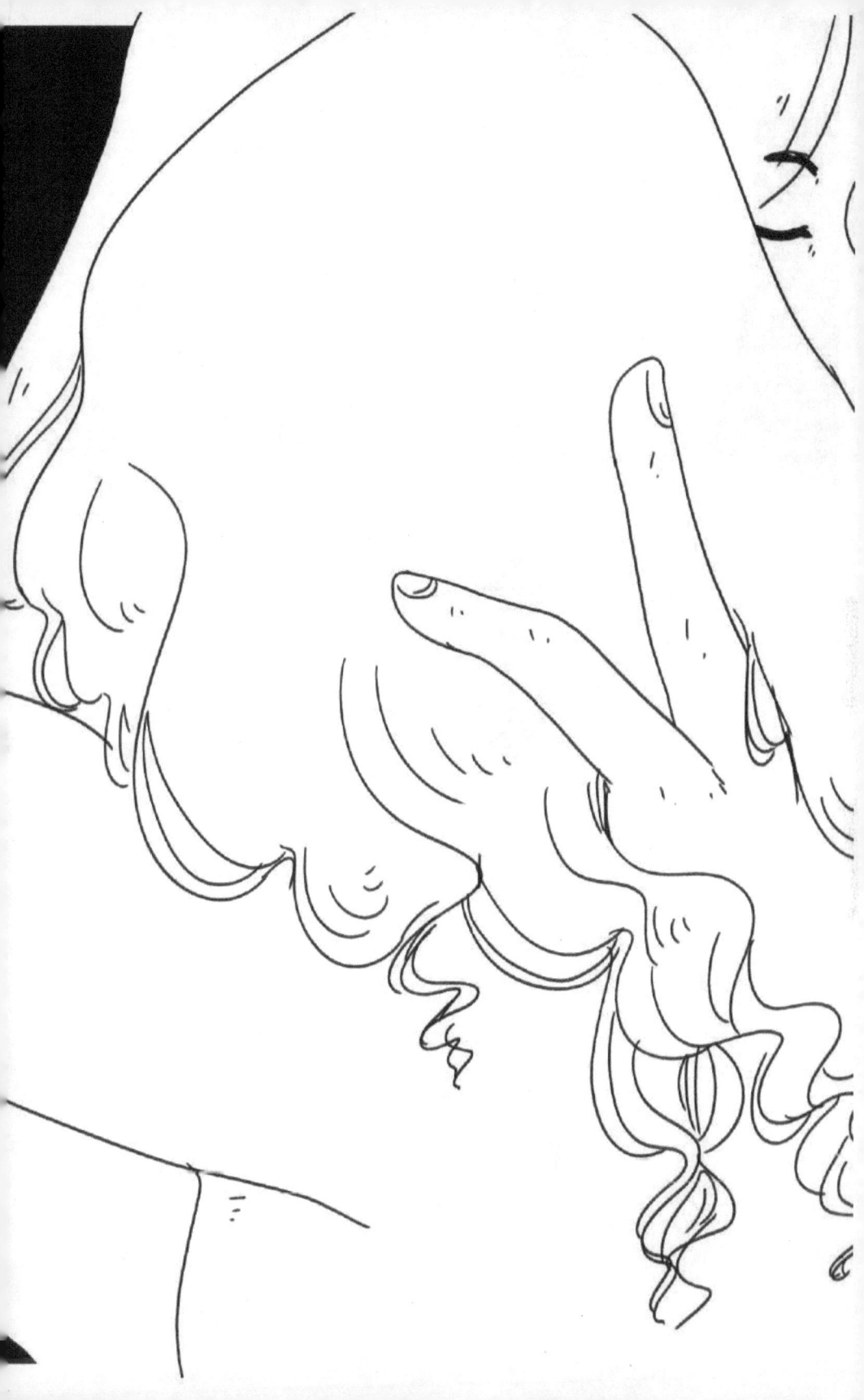

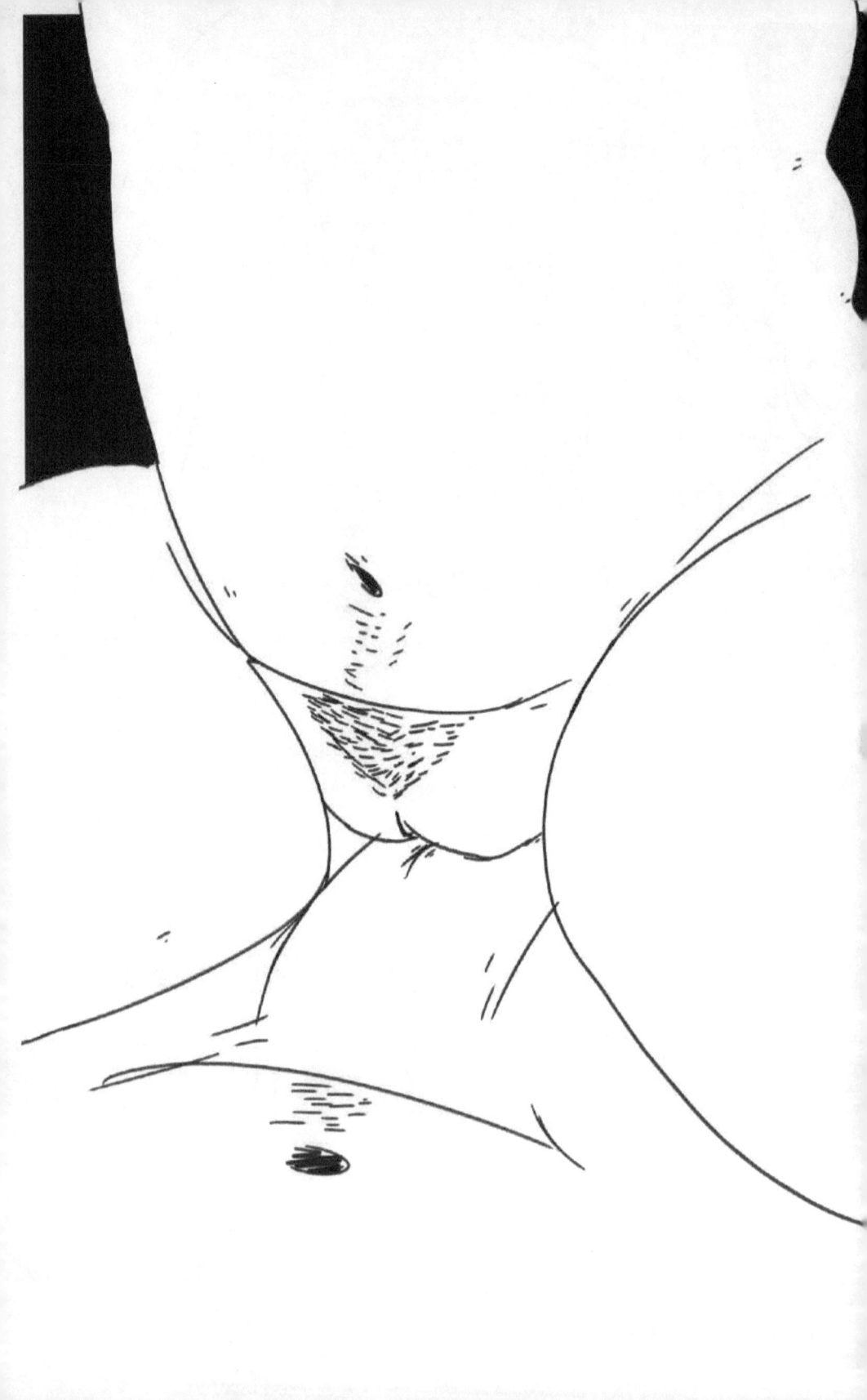

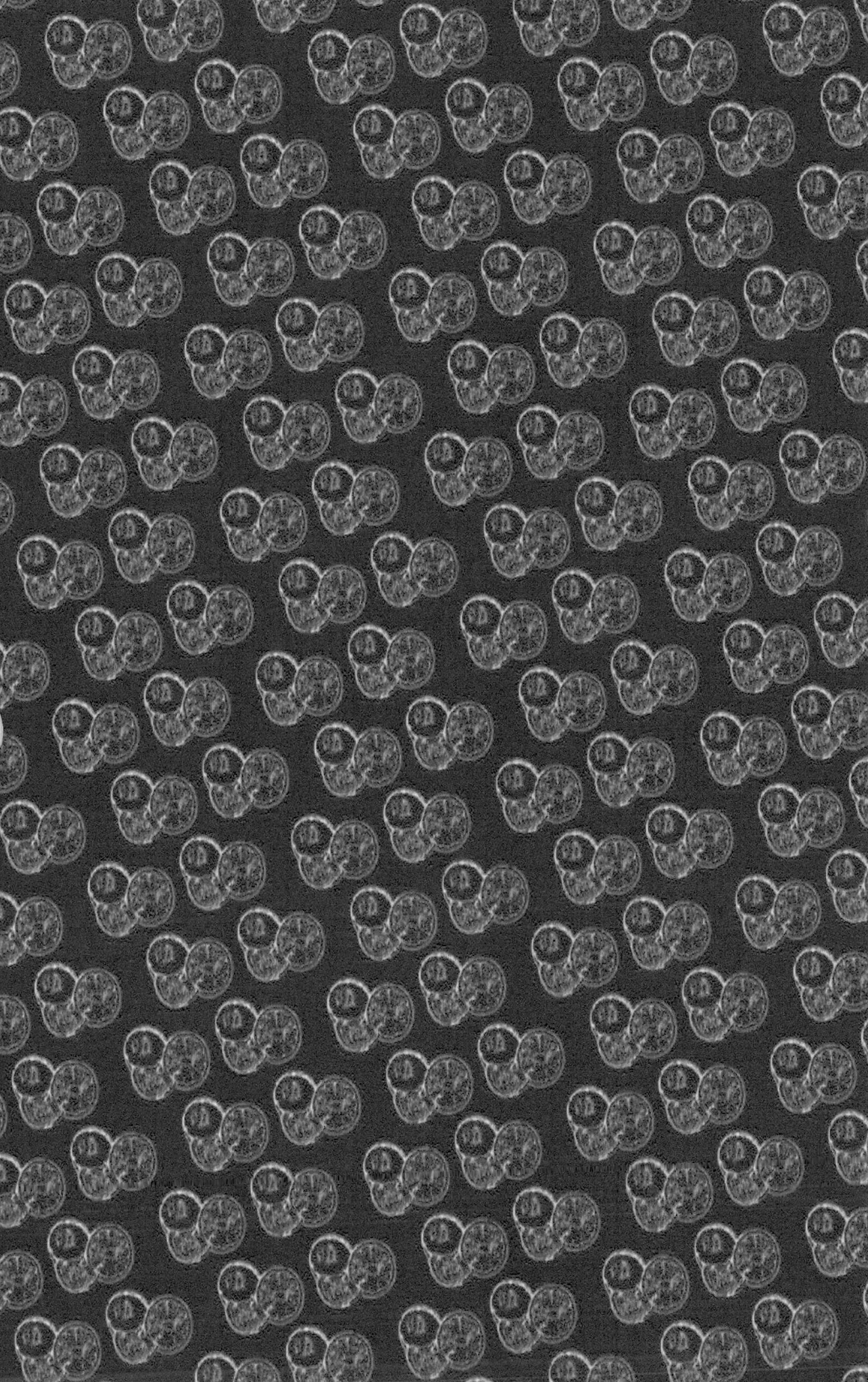

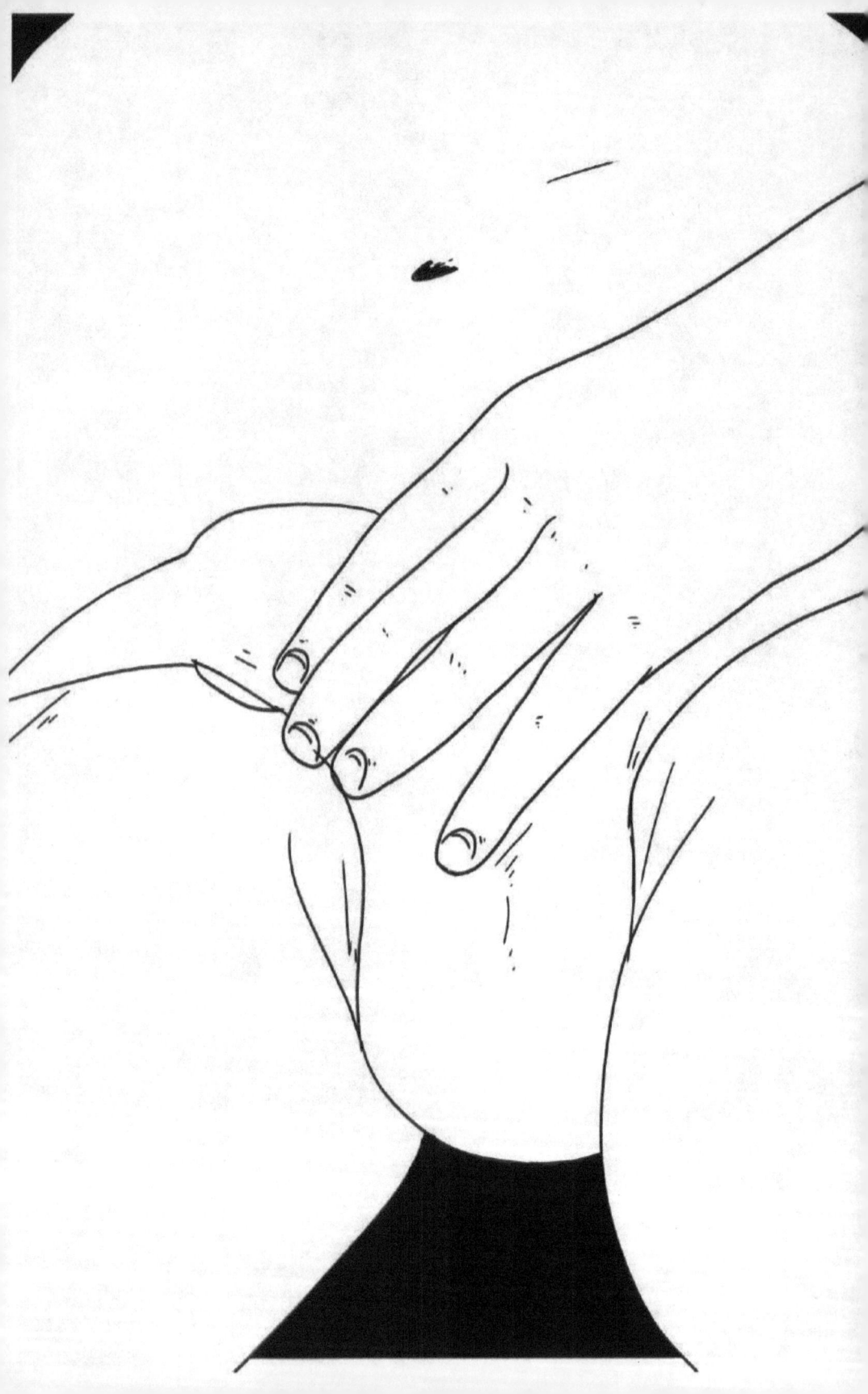

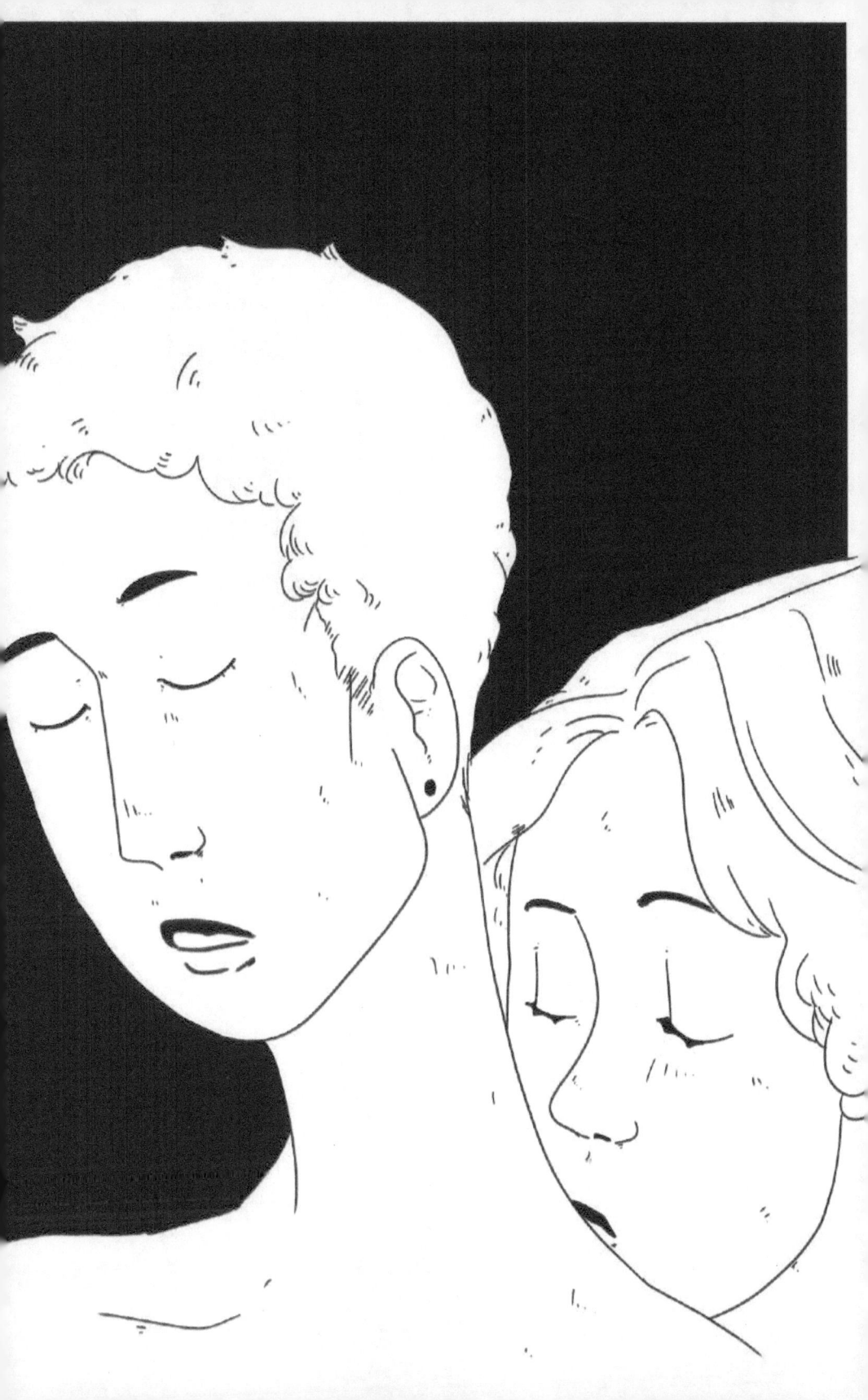

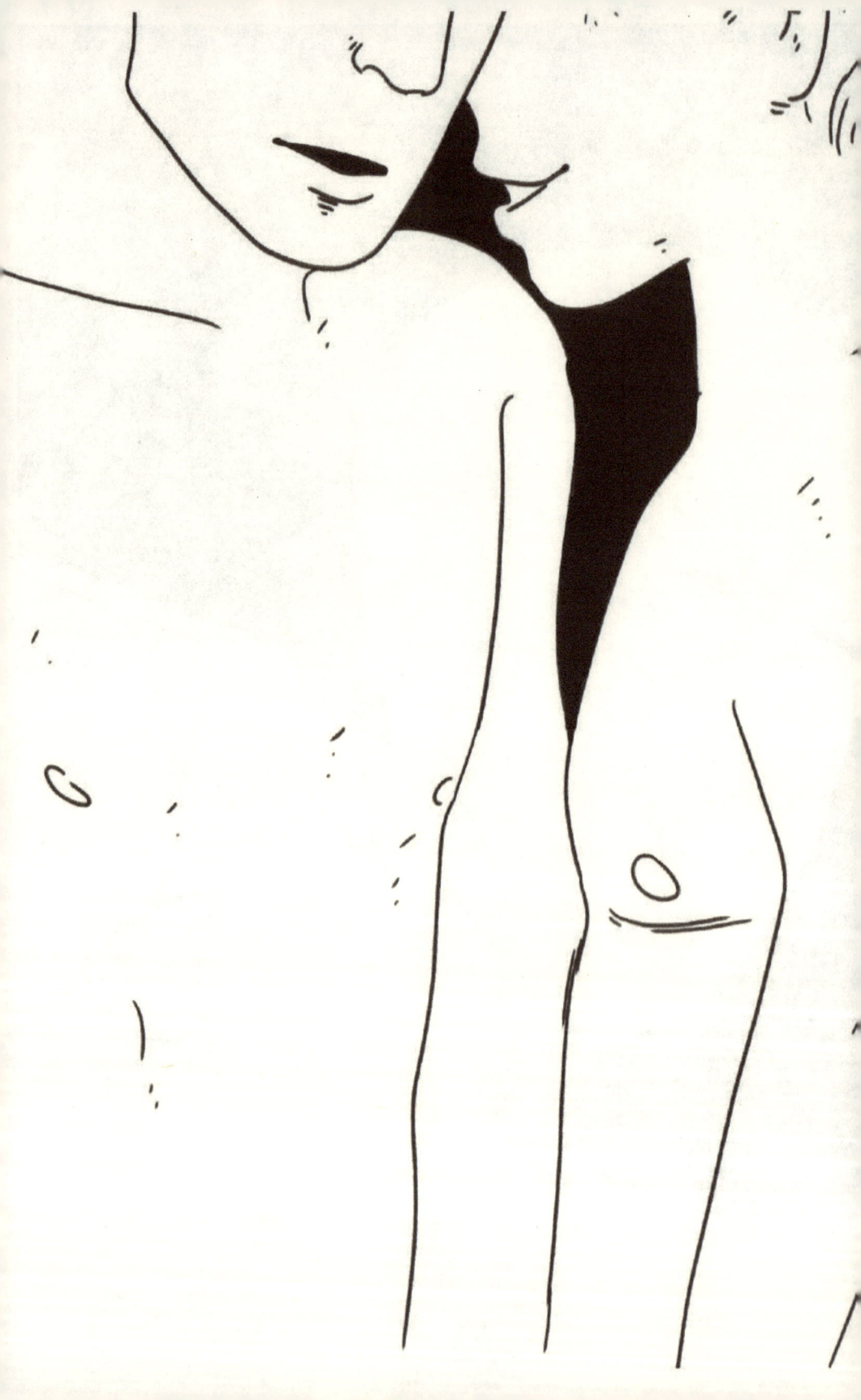

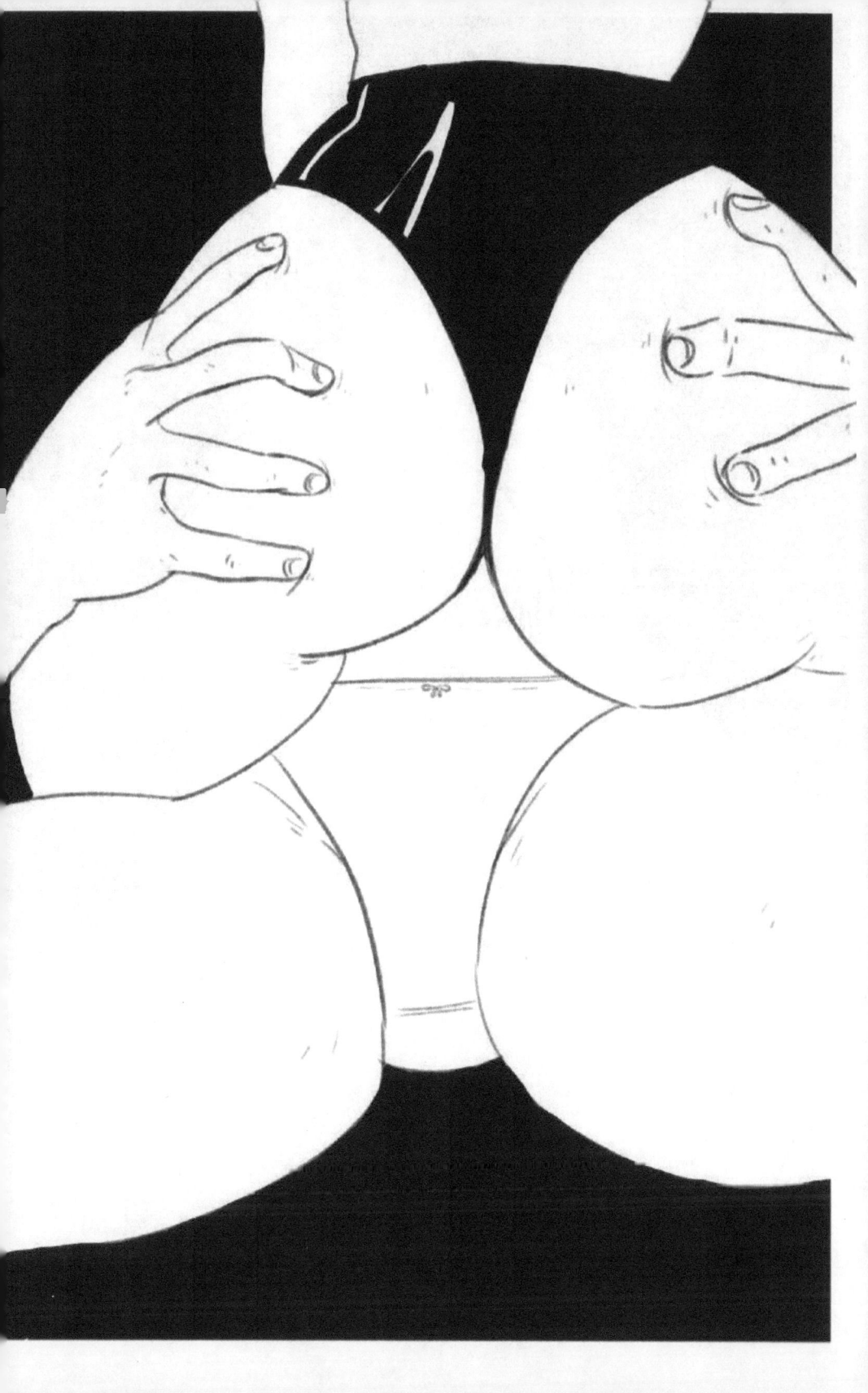

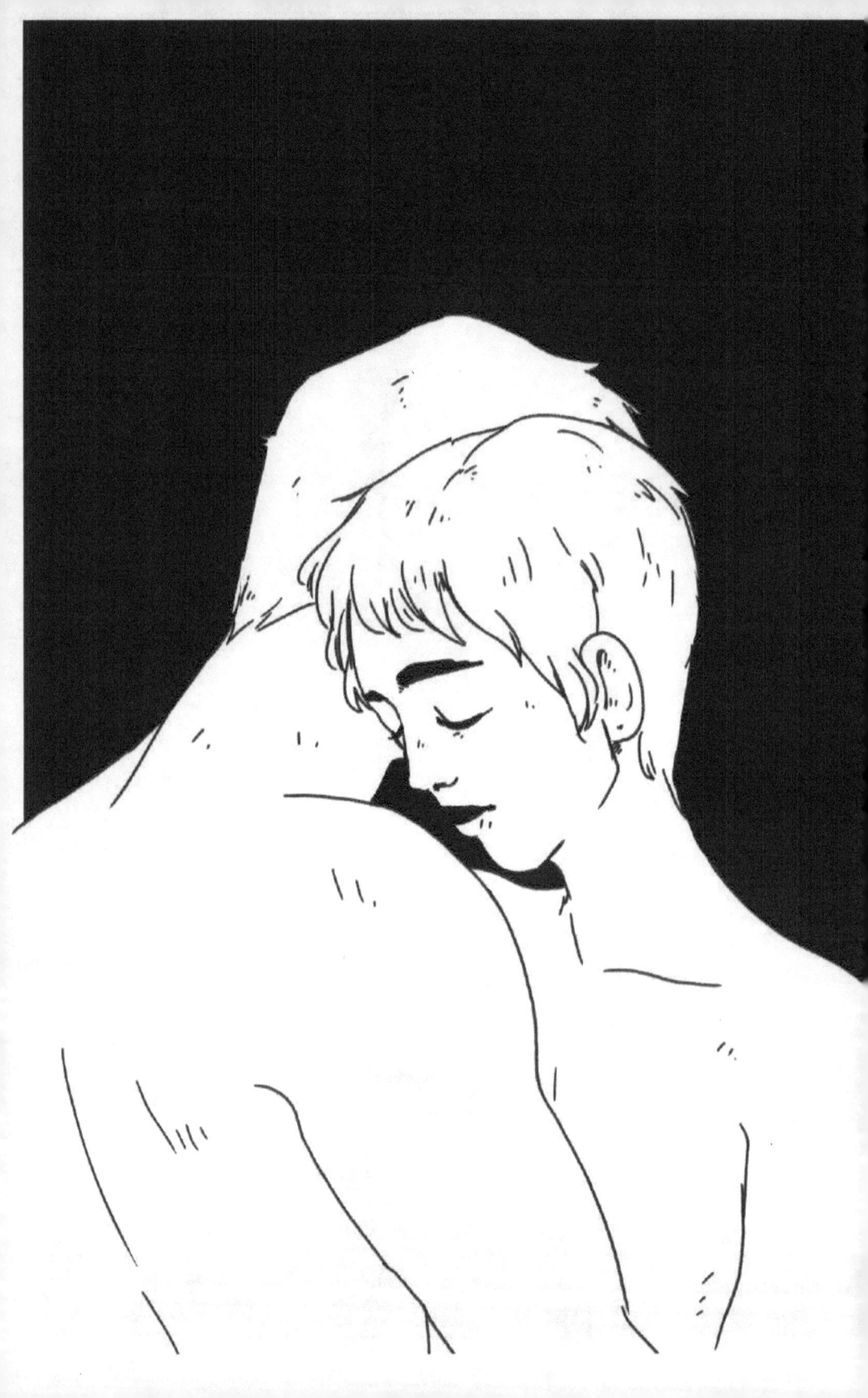

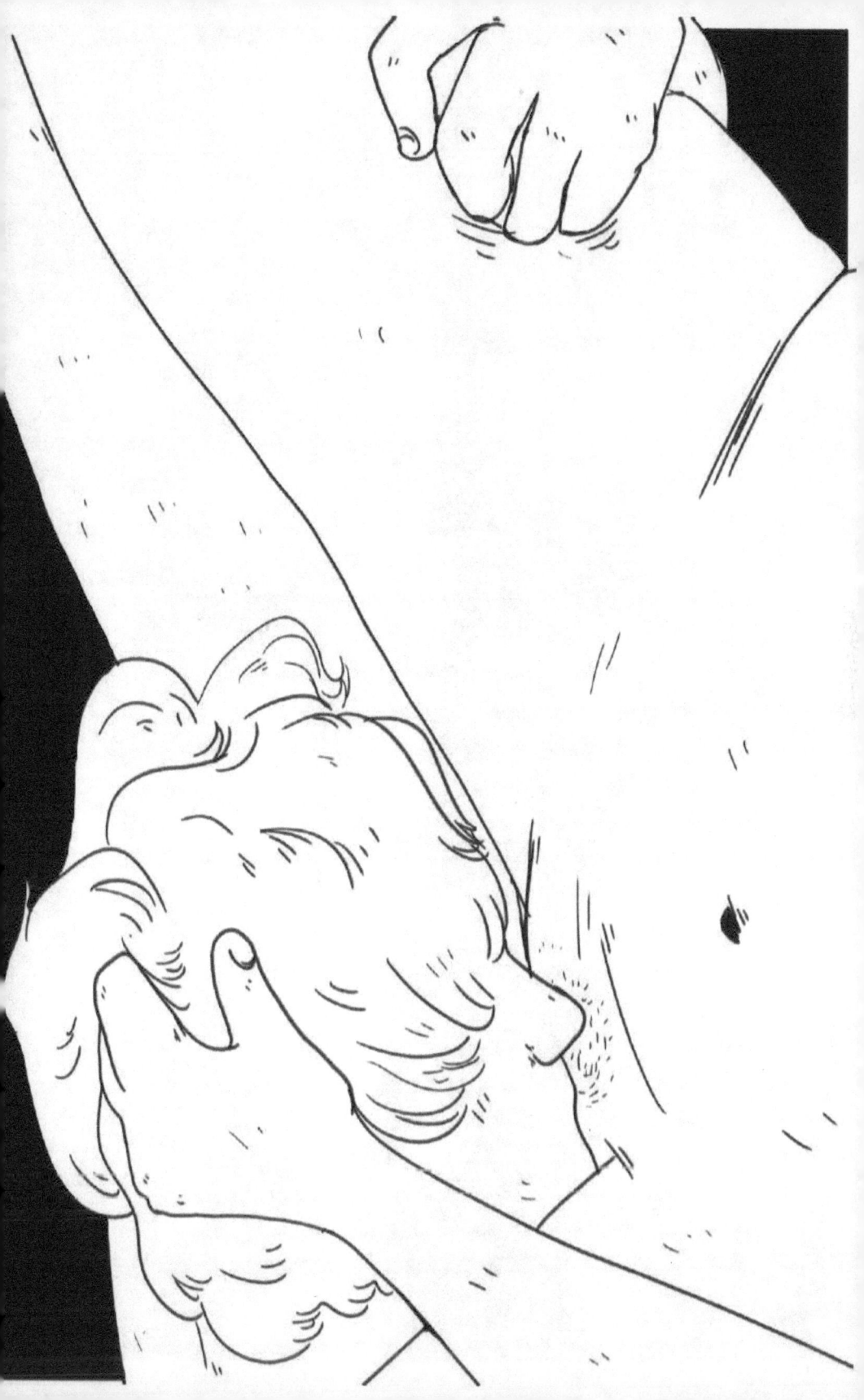

Hungry for more,
I sipped at the sweet juices
that remained
and plucked yet another
apple so that I, too,
could be wise

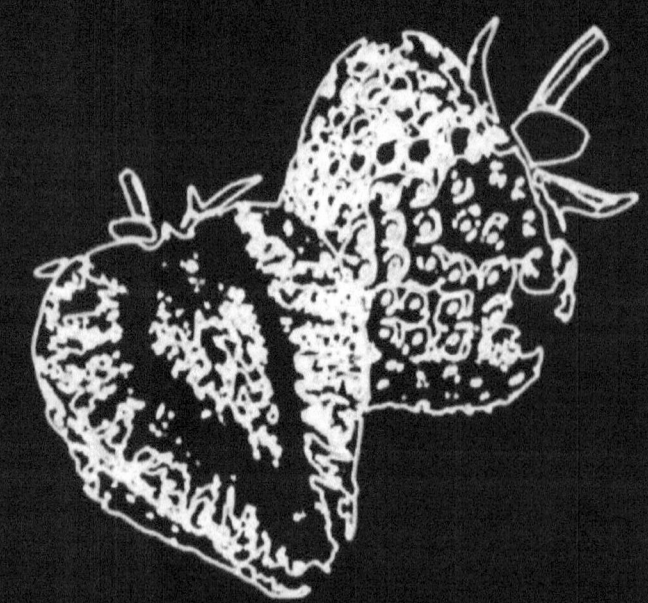

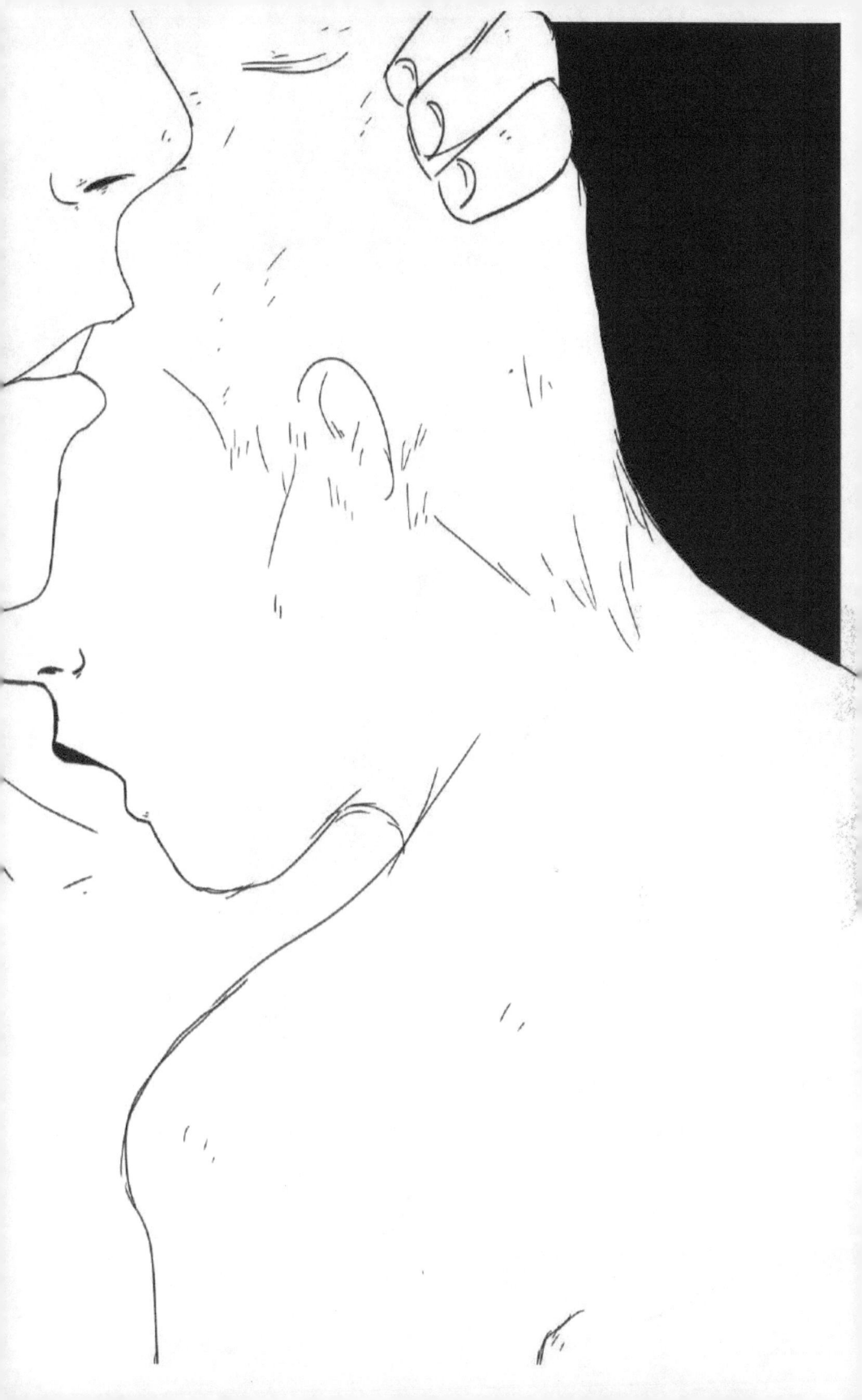

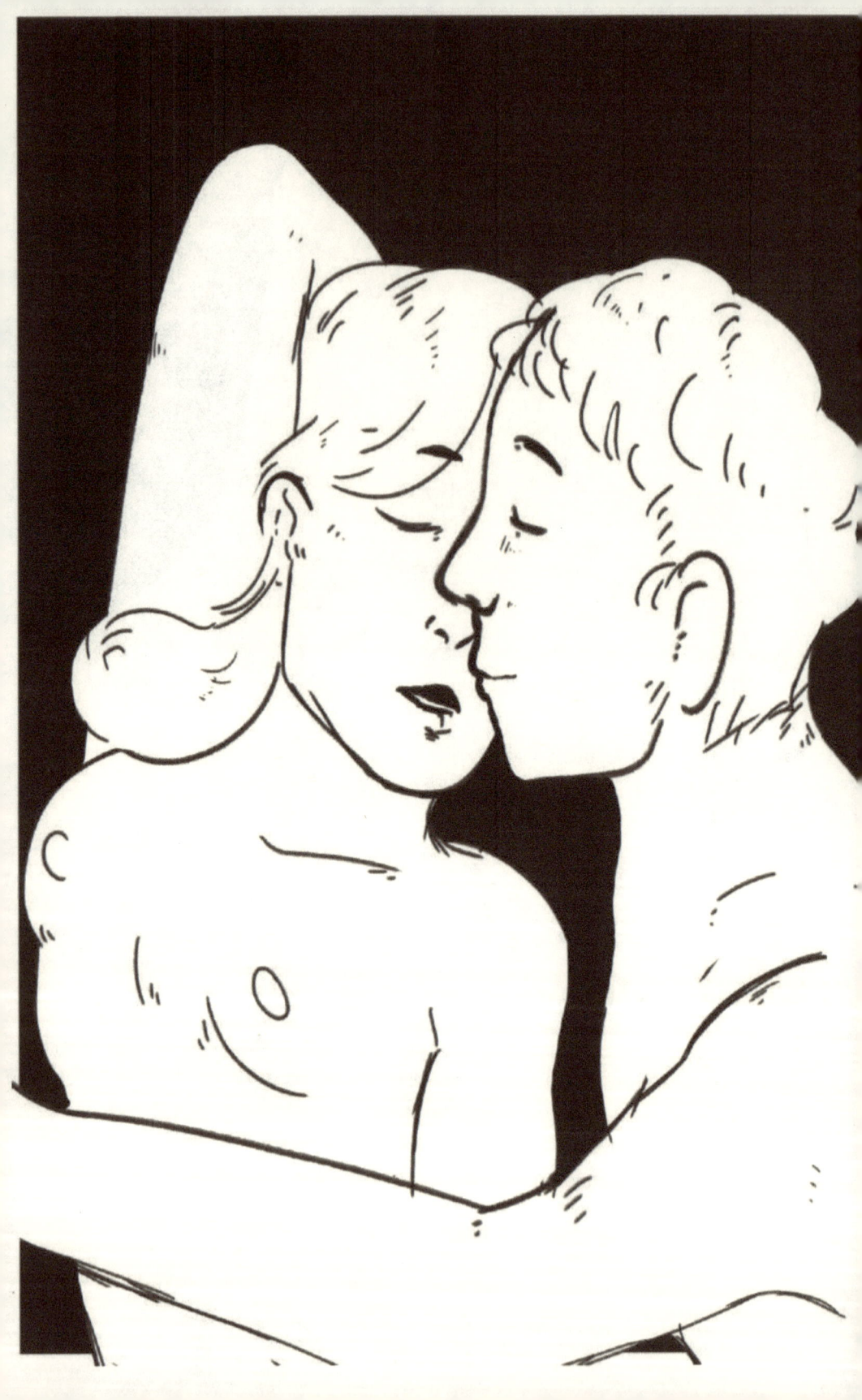

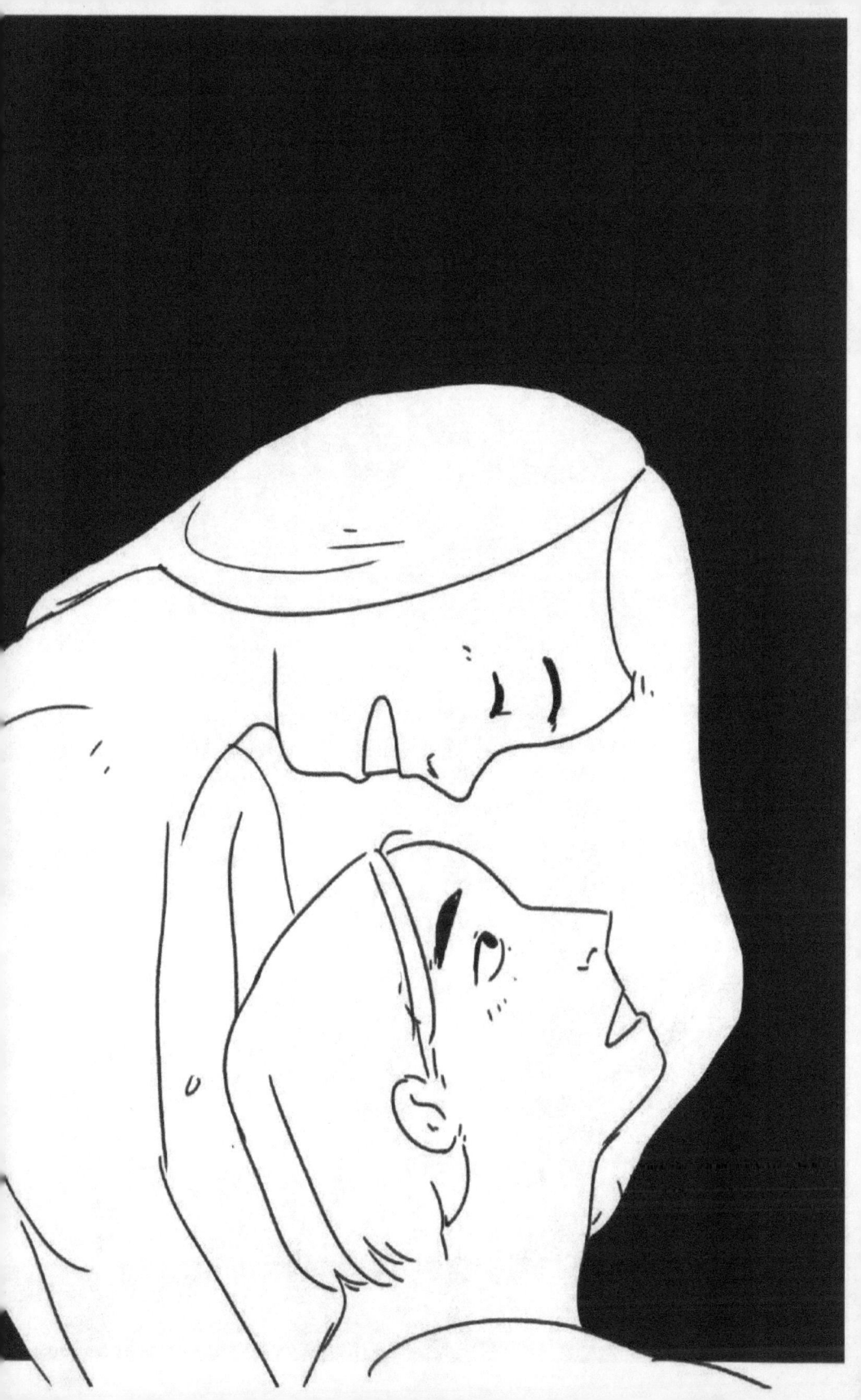

And on that Day
we felt love
real,true love
for the very first time

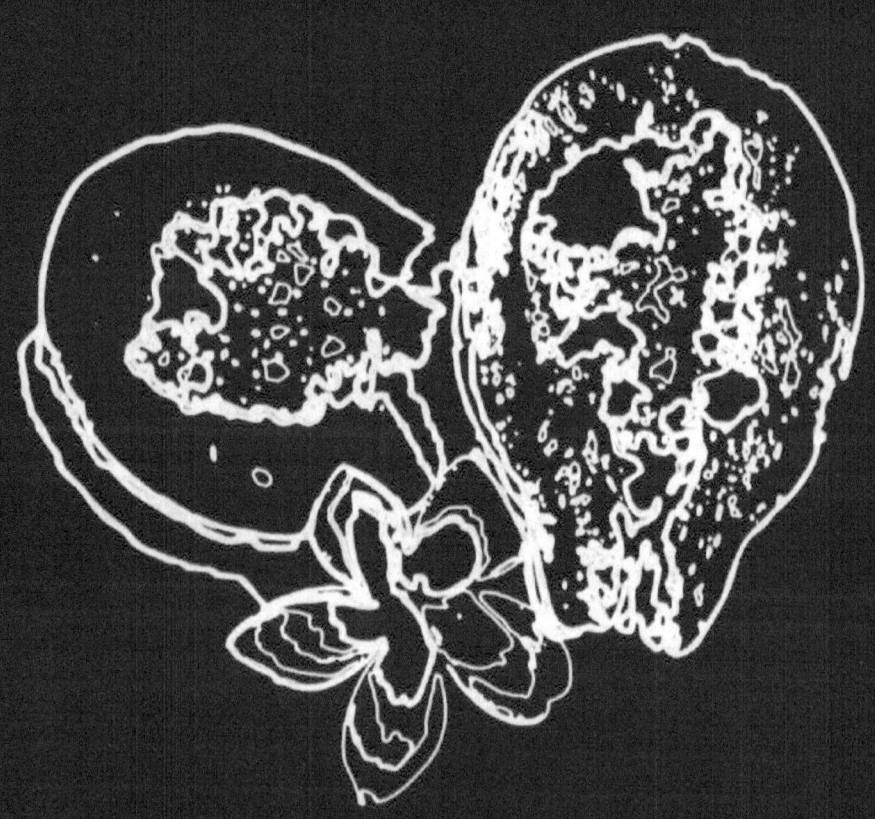

Inktober 2018

Jay Moss

@Angelpuns

Follow me on:
Tumblr
Instagram

Merch Available on
Society6

www.ingramcontent.com/pod-product-compliance
Lightning Source LLC
Chambersburg PA
CBHW021049180526
45163CB00005B/2347